Lake Erie

PENNSYLVANIA

River

Allegheny

Shippingport
Freedom
Sewickley
Pittsburgh
West Elizabeth

OHIO

Muskingum

Empire
Marine Ferry
Dilles Bottom
Belmont
Clarington
New Martinsville
Proctor
Sistersville
St. Mary's

Wheeling

Scioto River

River
Relpert
Hockingport
Reedsville
Long Racine
Pomeroy
Middleport
Cheshire
Addison
Gallipolis

Marietta
Reno
Parkersburg
Ravenswood
New Haven
Point Pleasant
Leon
Buffalo
Poca

Muskingum River

Monongahela River

Little Miami River

Miami River

New Richmond
Moscow
Chilo
Utopia
Higginsport
Ripley
Manchester
Wrightsville
Stout
Byrna
Vista

Augusta
Maysville

River

Vanceburg
Fullerton
Portsmouth
Greenup
Ironton
Proctorville
Athalia
Sheridan
Ashland
Catlettsburg

Licking

River

Big

Sandy

River

Huntington
Kenova
St. Albans
Dunbar
South Charleston
Marmet
Pratt

WEST

VIRGINIA

Cedar Grove

Kanawha River

The Ohio River Valley

N

0		100 miles

0		200 kilometers

OHIO RIVER VALLEY SERIES

Rita Kohn and William Lynwood Montell
Series Editors

HERE COMES THE
SHOWBOAT!

BETTY BRYANT

*Best wishes
Betty Bryant
1994*

THE UNIVERSITY PRESS OF KENTUCKY

Publication of this book was assisted by a grant from the Indiana Humanities Council.

Scholarly publisher for the Commonwealth,
serving Bellarmine College, Berea College, Centre
College of Kentucky, Eastern Kentucky University,
The Filson Club, Georgetown College, Kentucky
Historical Society, Kentucky State University,
Morehead State University, Murray State University,
Northern Kentucky University, Transylvania University,
University of Kentucky, University of Louisville,
and Western Kentucky University.

Editorial and Sales Offices: Lexington, Kentucky 40508-4008

Library of Congress Cataloging-in-Publication Data

Bryant, Betty
  Here comes the showboat! / Betty Bryant.
    p.   cm. — (Ohio River Valley series)
  ISBN 0-8131-1862-X :
  1. Billy Bryant's Showboat.   2. Showboats—History—20th century.
3. River life—Ohio River—History—20th century.   4. Bryant family.
I. Title. II. Series.
PN2293.S4B79   1994
792′.022—dc20   93-47998

This book is printed on acid-free recycled paper meeting
the requirements of the American National Standard
for Permanence of Paper for Printed Library Materials.

to

Manase, David, Michael, and Michaeline

(in order of their appearance)

CONTENTS

SERIES FOREWORD

The impact of the Ohio River in the context of the larger American story gained widespread public attention as a result of the "Always a River: The Ohio River and the American Experience" project sponsored by the National Endowment for the Humanities and the humanities councils of the states of Illinois, Indiana, Kentucky, Ohio, Pennsylvania, and West Virginia, with a mix of private and public organizations.

The Ohio River Valley Series, conceived and published by the University Press of Kentucky, extends the work of the Always a River project through the publication of an ongoing series of books that examine and illuminate the waterway, the land in its watershed, and the waves of people who made this fertile and desirable area their place of residence, of refuge, of commerce and industry, of cultural development and, ultimately, of engagement with American democracy.

The goal of the Always a River project has been to aid our understanding of the implications of change caused through natural and human interrelationships with the Ohio River. The unifying theme for the Ohio River Valley series carries forward this initial goal as each author contributes to a wider understanding of Ohio River Valley history and folklife. Each title's story is told through people interacting within their particular place and time. Each reveals why records, papers, and oral stories preserved by families and institutions offer rich resources for the history of the Ohio River and of the nation. Each traces the impact the river and its tributaries has had on individuals and cultures, and conversely how these individuals and cultures have made an impact on the valley as we know it.

The components of the Always a River project included:

• A floating exhibition on a specially fabricated barge that stopped at 21 sites along the Ohio River from May 22 to September 8, 1991.

• A book of seven essays and an introductory historical overview, *Always a River: The Ohio River and the American Experience* (Indiana University Press, 1991).

• A river-wide newspaper supplement containing seven articles that addressed current issues surrounding life and commerce along the Ohio.

• A Watercolors of the Ohio exhibition and catalog of juried paintings by artists associated with watercolor societies in the states along the Ohio.

• A valley-wide library reading/discussion program covering three themes: "Exploration, Encounters, and Change: The Ohio River and the Nation," "Heroes and Heroines of the Ohio River Valley," and "Landings: New Perspectives on Local History in the Ohio River Region."

• A valley-wide conference bringing together scholars and experts to examine the history and folklife of the Ohio River Valley.

• A series of locally developed educational initiatives.

Follow-up activities in addition to this Ohio River Valley series include plans for an Ohio River Heritage Corridor, continuation of library reading/discussion programs, biennial conferences on specific themes relevant to the Ohio River Valley, and a major new Falls of the Ohio Interpretive Center at Clarksville, Indiana.

In the process of being a river, the Ohio (and its tributaries) has touched us individually and collectively. This series celebrates the story of a valley through multiple voices and visions.

Kenneth L. Gladish
President and Executive Director
Indiana Humanities Council

PREFACE

The Ohio River Valley has a rich story to tell, in and of itself as a fascinating geologic, geographic entity and through diverse waves of inhabitants whose known residency spans from the withdrawal of the last great glaciers some 15,000 years ago up to the present. Each volume in the Ohio River Valley series illuminates an aspect of life along the Ohio, which stretches 981 miles from the confluence of the Allegheny and Monongahela (at Pittsburgh) to the confluence with the Mississippi (at Cairo) and along the multiple tributaries that together provide an inland waterway system connecting nearly one-third of the current mainland USA. Written by scholars and experts in various disciplines, these books engage readers in a discourse about the heritage and the future of the Ohio River Valley as it relates to the nation as a whole.

Here Comes the Showboat!, the second in the Ohio River Valley series, chronicles three generations of the Bryant family as they plied the Ohio and its tributaries from the turn of the century to World War II, tying up at landings in cities, towns, and settlements, to bring a uniquely American theatre to eager and loyal audiences.

The *Bryant's Showboat* grew out of a history of entertainment on the Ohio. In 1790, Fort Pitt had the first recorded theatrical performances along the Ohio River. The mess hall of the barracks was rearranged with tables serving as the stage and benches as seating.

Military men and their wives were the performers. Cincinnati, in 1801, is believed to have had the first theatre built or remodeled for putting on plays. Noah Ludlow is credited with opening the first "professional" Ohio River theatre season in a rented hall in Pittsburgh in 1815 and also the first theatre season in Louisville in 1816. Itinerant acting companies put on performances in rented spaces, bringing elaborate sets and costumes downriver as they traveled from landing to landing.

The first showboat—a flatboat one hundred feet long by sixteen feet wide—was built in Pittsburgh for the enterprising acting family headed by William Chapman. There is some evidence that the first season was 1831. Chapman's *Floating Theatre* started a tradition that has continued to the present, except during the Civil War. "Entertainment boats" on the Ohio waters and its tributaries ranged from the small shantyboats to the large floating palaces, presenting such diversions as museums, medicine shows, minstrels, merry-go-rounds, arcades, and portrait studios. Some were called "temples of amusement." They provided patrons with spectacle and glimpses of other worlds. For many, the showboats were the only source of the latest popular music and plays.

Since the early 1800s, the Ohio River has been the birthplace of well over one hundred showboats and other entertainment vessels. Some operations lasted only a few shows, but the more successful toured the inland waterways for more than thirty seasons. The *Majestic* at Cincinnati, originally built in 1923 near Pittsburgh by the Capt. Thomas J. Reynolds family, is perhaps the best preserved showboat. In 1990 the *Majestic* was designated a National Landmark.

In 1957, a refurbished Pittsburgh again spawned a new kind of river-based entertainment. One hundred twenty-five years after Chapman's showboat pushed off downriver, Robert Austin Boudreau's American Wind Symphony first brought a music barge to audiences the length of the Ohio and now tours along waterways of the world. Renamed the American Waterways Wind Orchestra and traveling in its specially designed floating arts center named *Point Counterpoint II*, this group merges the daring of early American enterprise with the best in contemporary arts.

Today showboats are specially outfitted vessels, permanently moored at their landings, delivering the same stock characters and plots that have delighted audiences since President Jackson's days.

Though other showboat books exist, this one provides an insightful catalog of life in the valley as well as an intimate glimpse into the art and economics of operating a floating theatre. Briskly told through family stories, personal remembrances, and a vast store of visual materials, *Here Comes the Showboat!* records the Ohio River's role in the larger story of American theatre.

Rita Kohn
William Lynwood Montell
Series Editors

INTRODUCTION

My father was Captain Billy Bryant and I was raised on his showboat. The floating theater was my home and the river was my back yard.

While other children were learning how to walk, I was learning how to swim, and I knew how to set a trotline, gig a frog, catch a crawfish, and strip the mud vein out of a carp by the time I was four.

Dad called me a river rat.

I always become homesick whenever I hear the song "Somewhere over the Rainbow," for that's where I used to live. And it *was* a place where troubles melted like lemon drops, and where "dreams that you dared to dream" really *did* come true!

I was born at the tail end of a unique and delightful era and raised on one of the last showboats to struggle for survival against the devastating crunch of progress.

Showboats came formally into being in 1831 when the Chapman family from England launched their first Floating Theater at Pittsburgh, Pennsylvania. Their heyday was in the first decade of the twentieth century when, along with a dozen or more smaller craft, huge boats like the *New Grand Floating Palace* with a thousand seats, the *Sunny South* with twelve hundred seats and the *Goldenrod* with a capacity of fourteen hundred were plying the inland streams.

Featuring a medley of melodrama and vaudeville, they brought laughter and therapeutic tears into the humdrum lives of isolated people who looked forward to their annual arrival as an excuse for an undeclared holiday. As one of the too few bits of indigenous Americana that we have in this country, it's a pity that the showboat's image has become so distorted. When thought of at all, it seems to be remembered as a near mythical craft which is part packet, part excursion, and part ferry boat.

It's surprising to many people that a typical showboat had no power of its own, no stern wheel, side wheel, motor, or engine. It was pushed from town to town by a steamboat tied to the stern. Equally surprising is the fact that it carried no paying passengers or freight. The only people who traveled on board were members of the family, cast, and crew.

A showboat was exactly what its name implies: a theater, built on a flat-bottomed barge for the express purpose of carrying entertainment to hundreds of thousands of river-bottom farmers along our water-bordered frontier. The larger municipalities had theaters, opera houses, and music halls, but between the cities were long stretches of rolling hills and deep green valleys, dotted with little hamlets and surrounding farms where the only social events were barn raisings, quilting bees, and corn huskings. These affairs, which in reality were merely difficult chores made lighter by sharing, were widely separated by weeks of back-breaking labor. Every day, each member of the family rose before the sun and went to bed soon after its last rays left the sky, often to dream, not surprisingly, of the showboat. These lighted giants were glorious interruptions in the monotony of their work-filled lives, and sometimes farmers and their families followed them up or down the river for two or three performances, loath to have the magic slip away.

Eventually, nearly a dozen gigantic, ornate, and costly showboats were in serious competition with each other, and their mad scramble for choice locations and larger audiences resembled nothing as much as a feeding frenzy of sharks. In trying to best each other, they had outpriced themselves. Some of them began playing larger towns

to meet their soaring operational costs, but when they met with only modest financial improvement, many of their owners thought the showboat era was over.

They had forgotten one very important fact. The showboat was originally intended for the hinterland, and the smaller ones, like ours, would continue for many more years, floating along at a leisurely pace totally out of tempo with the rest of the world.

Even when radio and motion pictures would begin to compete for audiences, the little boats, being a good ten years behind the times, would continue to exist. They would draw back, like forest creatures, deeper into the sanctuary of weeds and willows that lined the banks of the cool, comforting backwaters.

Mainly family-operated, with low overheads and modest prices, they would go on for some time delivering the wholesome product that they advertised as

"Family entertainment, BY families, FOR families!"

CAST, BRED ON THE WATERS

When I was born, the showboat was tied up for the winter at West Elizabeth, Pennsylvania, on the Monongahela River, about twenty miles up from Pittsburgh.

In 1922, on the third of March, my mother carried me down the riverbank, over the stageplank, and onto my new home. I was ten days old. She crossed the deck and hurried through the front door to our living quarters.

My father, Captain Billy Bryant, rushed in just as she deposited me in the top tray of a prop trunk. In later years, mother would tell me that he looked at me and said, "She's beautiful, Josie! We'll open the season with *Uncle Tom's Cabin*, and Eliza can carry her across the ice!"

Dad was true to his word. At the age of six weeks, I began my theatrical career in the arms of the fleeing slave. In my baby book, which mother kept with the zeal of Saint Peter, a footnote informs that I never cried during a performance. In spite of rough handling and the bedlam created by barking dogs and shouting men, I cooed, gurgled, and smiled, happy and content with my role in life.

The footlights warmed me like a giant incubator, and instead of mouthing a pacifier, I stared contentedly into the bright border lights overhead. I used the cold barrel of a prop gun for my teething ring, and the crowd's laughter was my lullaby. I was the epitome of

The Bryant Family (*left to right*):
Josephine, Violet, Sam, Florence, Billy, and Betty

the born-in-a-trunk baby, and my every waking moment was filled
with attention, training, and care.

To Mother, who had just enough maternal instinct to keep from
eating her young, I was a delightful new toy. She carried me with her
at all times, securely strapped into a clever contraption called an Oriole Basket, a wicker buggy that was pushed along on two wheels. In

response to a sharp pull on the handle, the wheels would retract and the buggy could be stood on the floor or carried over one arm. It was made by a company in Cincinnati and sold under the slogan of "Take Baby Wif Oo!" It had a remarkable effect on my life.

Mother began teaching me how to talk even before I could sit up, and, as I was (thanks to the Oriole Basket) constantly at her side, my tutoring was rarely interrupted. From morning till night I was under

Betty at 14 months:
"Roses on my shoulders"

the spell of her gentle, hypnotic voice, and the result was truly strange. I have been told by many people that by the time I was nine months old I could both recite and read the alphabet from A to Z as well as spell hippopotamus and octopus. Witnesses to this phenomenon were plentiful, for Mother never missed an opportunity to show me off.

The following season, when the boats opened, I was fourteen months old, and Mother dressed me in a satin dress, trimmed with rose buds, a matching hat, long white stockings, and black patent leather shoes. Then, she gently pushed me out in front of the curtain, where I lisped to a surprised but delighted audience,

> Roses on my shoulders,
> Slippers on my feet.
> I'm my daddy's darling.
> Don't you sink my feet?

Mother said that the last line was supposed to be "Don't you think I'm sweet?" but she never corrected me.

The hula

Betty, age three, in costume for
performing the black bottom

Dressed to perform
George M. Cohan's "Great
Easter Sunday Parade"

From then on, I was a regular part of the show and never missed a performance. Mother's scrapbook is cluttered with pictures of me doing impressions of George M. Cohan, Al Jolson, Eddie Cantor, and George S. Primrose. There are snapshots of me in appropriate costumes for the soft shoe, a buck dance, the Charleston, the black bottom, and the waltz clog. In one picture, I'm doing a hula in a rather worse-for-wear grass skirt that my pet rabbit had found irresistible.

My favorite specialty was a song and dance to a George M. Cohan number. I wore a pink satin dress with a matching cloche hat. The skirt had flower-trimmed inserts with a ribbon running from each side of the hem to a bow tied to my wrist. I carried a big, stuffed, pink rabbit and a ruffled umbrella and sang:

> Dressed in my best in my new Easter gown,
> I took a stroll to the best part of town.
> There, with the richest beside me,
> They eyed me the moment they spied me.
> Fashionable folks all started to stare,
> At my 'most perfect "Park Avenue air."
> Little they dreamed me from West Chester Square,
> As I Marched along, with the joyous throng
> In the great Easter Sunday parade.

Then, after a chorus of dancing the waltz clog, I would stroll off, singing the last two lines again:

> I marched along, with the joyous throng
> In the great Easter Sunday parade.

Perhaps it was my favorite number because of the frilly costume. Mother made all of my wardrobe and usually dressed me in a boy's outfit, a Yama suit (a one-piece, traditional clown suit with a neck ruff and pom-poms down the front), or some character costume. When Charles Lindbergh made his solo flight across the Atlantic Ocean, we did a production number in his honor. Before you could say, "Hooray for the red, white and blue!" mother had whipped up

Betty on the front deck of the *Valley Belle*, in her military tap costume

"Lucky Lindy"

an aviator's suit with a helmet and goggles that made me look like a plucked owl. As a finishing touch, around my neck she wrapped a six-foot scarf that dragged behind me on the floor. When the curtain went up, the full cast was on stage. They were all dressed in white, waving little American flags and singing:

> Lindbergh, oh what a flying fool was he,
> Lindbergh, his name will live in history.
> Over the ocean, he flew all alone,
> Gambling with fate and with dangers unknown.

At the end of the song, the rest of the cast would step to the side and leave me in center stage. Fighting with the entangled scarf, I would struggle through a military tap dance. Then we would all march in place, singing another chorus together.

As we neared the end of the song, everyone walked downstage toward the audience, and behind us a giant American flag unrolled from the ceiling, scattering diamond dust over everything. As red flares were lighted in the wings, pinwheels nailed to each side of the proscenium arch would begin to spin and my grandfather would enter dressed as Uncle Sam. In a frenzy of patriotic excitement, I would jump up and down in tempo with the music and scream the last lines of the song,

> Take off your hats to plucky, lucky Lindbergh,
> The eagle of the U.S.A.!!!

That was in 1927, a great year for Lindbergh and an equally great year for me. Of course, his triumph was planned, mine was the result of a near disaster I caused.

Besides singing and dancing between acts, behind the scenes, I pulled curtains, flickered lights, and furnished sound effects from the greenroom. For a rifle shot, I slapped a broom handle on a table and put-a-thumped two coconut shell halves against the wall to simulate horses' hooves. For a storm, I rattled the long strip of tin called a thunder-sheet and cranked a wind machine. I screamed and moaned for off-stage victims and dropped a crash box to simulate breaking glass. But my favorite job was operating the snow-cradle.

A snow-cradle is made of two long, thin strips of wood called battens with a two-foot-wide strip of muslin nailed between them. The muslin is perforated with staggered slits about four inches in length. Before the show, the cradle, or muslin is carefully loaded, or filled with small squares of white paper. The battens are brought together and are attached to the ceiling. Two ropes run from the ends of the battens, over pulleys and down the off-stage wall. A gentle tug on the ropes agitates the cradle and allows the particles of white paper gradually to fall free and float gently down like snowflakes behind a window built into the set.

One night we were playing *Way Down East*. I was at my post, and the snow was falling slowly but steadily outside the window. The blue light, which gave the illusion of night, seemed to have a mesmeric effect on me, and soon, I became caught up in the action of the play. I began to cry. Instinctively, I clung to the rope, and snow fell faster. Soon I was sobbing convulsively and jerking the rope with each sob. The snow began falling in clumps, the confused audience started to titter, and the actors began to talk louder. The louder they talked the harder I cried, and the harder I cried the faster the snow fell.

By now, the snow was cascading down on both sides of the window, and the actors found themselves standing ankle-deep in it. By the time they dropped the curtain and loosened my death grip on the rope, the cast was furious, the audience was roaring, and I was in hysterics. A lesser producer would have fired me on the spot. Dad merely kicked me upstairs, changed the show to *East Lynne*, and put me to work in earnest playing the part of Little Willie. I was ecstatic!

Many of the old melodramas featured a child. In *East Lynne*, there was Little Willie, in *Uncle Tom's Cabin*, Little Eva, and in *Ten Nights in a Barroom*, Mary Morgan, the daughter of the village drunkard. In each of these plays, the child dies and, even more morbidly, the child's death seems to solve all the problems of the play.

In *Uncle Tom's Cabin*, when Little Eva died, St. Claire freed the slaves; in *Ten Nights in a Barroom*, when Mary Morgan died, her father quit drinking; and in *East Lynne*, when Little Willie died, his estranged parents were reconciled.

Eventually, I would play each of these parts, and by the time I was eight I had died in practically every town on the inland waterway. Of course, I still worked props and painted scenery and tied cotton on the bushes for the slaves to pick. I even rattled the thunder sheet and cranked the wind machine. But it was many years before they let me near the snow-cradle.

HOME
SWEET SHOWBOAT

All showboats were built on approximately the same floorplan and ours was no exception. From the pilot house to the hull, it looked like a little square box on top of a shoebox that was built on a flat-bottomed barge.

Roofed decks which we called porches, both upstairs and down, extended from each end, and between them, little walkways known as guards ran along the entire length of the boat on either side of the auditorium. Posts that rose from the lower deck to the roof were spaced along these guards and held protective horizontal planks called guardrails.

Windows were scattered evenly on both levels, and between them the name of the boat was spelled out in letters four feet high. Around the pilot house, along the roof, and on the edge of the middle guard were hundreds of light bulbs. When the generator was turned on at night the boat lit up like a floating fairyland.

In the center of the lower front deck a set of double doors opened onto a short passageway which led to the auditorium. To the left was Mother and Dad's living quarters, where I slept in a trunk until I was old enough to have my own room, to the right an office where tickets were sold through a window to people lining up on the porch.

Halfway down the aisle, wide stairs led off to the right. At the

Josephine and baby Betty on Violet's porch on *Bryant's New Showboat*, 1922

top they forked, the right branch leading to my grandparents' rooms, the left to the balcony.

There were twelve rows of seats in the back of the balcony and from these, along each wall, a small runway with a waist-high railing stretched all the way to the stage. A single row of theater seats was bolted along each side with their backs to the wall.

My grandparents' quarters consisted of a tiny bedroom and a large sitting room that ran the full width of the boat. It opened onto an equally spacious porch furnished with benches, chairs, and tables made of twisted willows by clever shantyboat craftsmen along the Big Sandy River and purchased for fifty cents apiece.

A green and white awning kept the sun from the wild ferns that were planted in large wooden tubs. Bird cages hung from the ceiling, their bottoms covered with clean, white sand from the sandbars

The auditorium in *Bryant's New Showboat,* filled to capacity

The greenroom behind the stage

along the route. In them, canaries perched and sang from dawn to dusk.

On the main floor of the theater the seats were divided into sections, two seats to a row on each side and seven to a row in the middle except for the first row, which had eight. Two aisles ran the length of the eighteen rows, and numbers were painted on the floor to correspond with numbers on the reserved seat tickets. General admission consisted of twelve rows of tiered seats in the back, under the balcony.

The floor slanted downward to the rear of the boat where the stage sat, approximately four feet high with a proscenium arch opening of eighteen feet. The stage was flanked by two boxes, four seats to a box. Between them was the orchestra pit. A door led from the pit to the hull under the stage where the concessions were stored.

At the rear of the stage, a short ladder ascended to the greenroom, where props were kept and quick changes of wardrobe made. A shelved cupboard held a goodly assortment of whistles, noisemakers, makeup, and wigs, and on hooks around the wall there were coats, hats, black snake whips, feather boas, and fur pieces.

On either end of the greenroom a door led to each side of the stage. Along the backstage passage the walls were lined with wooden pegs to which ropes, holding the curtains, were tied. In one corner, a switchboard afforded control of the lights. The switches were numbered, and a corresponding chart, pasted at the side, listed houselights, footlights, borders, reds, blues, baby spots.

At the front of the stage, just behind the prosceneum arch, was a roll curtain. It was painted to look like drapes behind a seascape in an oval frame. Four feet behind this was another roll curtain with a street scene on it. When the first curtain was up, the space between the street scene and the footlights was referred to as "in one." It was used for short exterior scenes or for vaudeville specialties between acts.

Behind the street scene, painted canvas tied to battens furnished appropriate backdrops. Flats, or "wings," stood three to a

The showboat stage

side, anchored by slots in the floor and a slotted board at the top which extended from the wall.

Flats are light wooden frames about the size of a tall door and covered with canvas. Reversible, ours were painted on one side with bushes and leaves for exteriors and on the other with simulated wood paneling for interiors. To change a set while either of the front roll curtains was down, actors, who doubled as stagehands, merely had to drop a back curtain, slide the wings out, turn them around, and slide them back into place.

Behind the stage, above the greenroom, were two bedrooms. One was kept available for my Aunt Florence's sporadic visits and the other belonged to me. Their doors opened onto the rear porch.

From my window I could see our steamboat, the *Valley Belle*. She was a beautiful old stern-wheeler with a deep-throated whistle that was known all along the inland waterways.

The two boats were fastened together with ratchet chains, and both boats were steered from the showboat pilot house with long tiller lines running from the pilot wheel to the rudders on the stern of the steamboat. The pilot signaled to the engineer by means of whistle cords and bell ropes.

Besides the members of our family, we carried four or five actors and a crew to run the steamboat. Dad had his own pilot's papers from the head of the Allegheny to the upper Mississippi, but we also had an engineer, a fireman, a deckhand, a cabin boy, and a cook.

While the family lived on the showboat, the other actors and the steamboat crew lived on the *Valley Belle*. Crew members slept in cots on the main deck, which held the boiler room, engine room, and coal bins. Upstairs, on the misnamed boiler deck, the actors occupied staterooms that flanked a corridor running from the pilot house to the dining room and galley at the stern.

Because the boats were always moved early in the morning, before the wind rose, the crew was served coffee and homemade doughnuts or fritters at 4:30 A.M., but, to accommodate the late-rising actors, breakfast was available until ten, by which time the boats were tied up at a new landing.

There was a constant feud between actors and crew on the showboat. At night, when the members of the crew were trying to sleep, the actors kept them awake. In the morning, the crew, rising early, disturbed the actors, who liked to sleep late.

Dinner was served at noon and supper at five. Everyone was called to meals by the clanging of a giant bell that hung between the smokestacks on the upper deck. The food was served family-style with heavy white ironstone bowls of steaming fresh vegetables and platters of meat that Dad bought at local stores wherever we tied up. Often we had fresh fish caught by the actors, and the room always smelled of warm bread and rich, strong coffee.

The dining room held three tables, one small one for the members of the crew, another for actors, and a third for the family. They were all covered with red and white checkered oilcloth and set with oversized salt and pepper shakers, sugar bowls, mustard and catsup bottles, and glass spoon holders filled with teaspoons.

One of the duties of the cabin boy was to see that these containers were always well filled. His other responsibilities consisted of keeping the galley and dining room clean, mopping the floor daily, scrubbing the barrel that held our drinking water, and washing dishes with water that he pulled from the river with a draw bucket and heated on the back of the old cast-iron stove.

He was expected to keep the woodbox filled with dry driftwood from the riverbank and the coal bucket with coal from the boiler room on the main deck. He was to empty the ashes, light the fire, set the tables, peel potatoes, scrape vegetables, serve the meals, go with Dad for groceries, fetch ice, empty the icebox pan, march in the parade, and sometimes do a bit part in a play. For all this he received the magnificent sum of five dollars a week plus room and board.

The cabin boy was under the command of the cook, who ruled with a despotic hand, but the cook was under the even more autocratic command of my grandmother, who at an early date had appointed herself sole and supreme supervisor of the galley.

LADY VIOLET

Grandmother called herself "Lady Violet" and that is how she was addressed by actors and crew members. She took great pride in her American citizenship papers, but she spoke the King's English until the day she died. It was fascinating to listen to her adding and subtracting H's indiscriminately.

Violet was built like a pouter pigeon, and each morning she slipped into a pleated or draped dark silk dress and added a brooch or a rope of pearls. On her feet she wore pumps of soft kid or patent leather with Cuban heels. After carefully applying her makeup, she spent a great deal of time fussing with her reddish-brown hair, teasing and tormenting it into a frenzied mass of writhing ringlets.

As soon as the boats were landed she would begin fluttering around the porch like an obese hummingbird. Singing softly to herself, she would water the plants and wedge apple slices between the bars of the bird cages. After that she would receive the cook. Together, they would go over the menus for the day. Then the cook would retire to the kitchen and Lady Violet would make out the grocery list for my father. If she had her way, we would have eaten mutton and brussels sprouts at every meal. But, though Dad went through the daily ritual to please her, once in the village, he was prone to buy with an eye for bargains, heavily influenced by the territory, the season and, sometimes, unforeseen windfalls.

One spring at Ambrosia, West Virginia, on the Kanawha River, the annual flood arrived a little earlier than usual and caught the storekeeper totally unprepared. As a result, his shelves, laden with canned goods, were submerged for a good six days. All of the labels washed off and floated out the door. When the water receded, he was left with stacks of cans filled with no one knew what. He sold them off for a penny a can.

Dad bought two dollars' worth, and for a while, to the actors' disgust and my delight, every meal contained a certain element of surprise. For one whole week we ate peaches instead of vegetables. It was beef, potatoes, and peaches; pork, potatoes, and peaches; fish, potatoes, and peaches; chicken, potatoes, and peaches. Then, for a while, hominy kept showing up instead of dessert.

The mining towns of Pennsylvania offered us ingredients for goulash, stuffed cabbage, and borsch. The Tennessee gave us opossum and coon. The Ohio Valley smothered us in apples, corn, chicken, and what one cook called "fresh garden sass." Up the Kentucky River we were in game country, so rabbit, doves, squirrels, quail, and grouse found their way to the galley. The Mississippi Delta offered us crawfish, okra, cane, and spices. Up the Illinois, where the commercial fishermen set trotlines by the dozen, we served every kind of freshwater fare from catfish to turtle eggs.

Every afternoon at three o'clock, Lady Violet served tea. She would invite two or three of the actors, my mother and me. Of course, my grandfather Sam would be there as well. We would all gather on the porch to enjoy bread and butter with blackberry preserves and mint jelly or tiny cress sandwiches.

It was all quite formal, and, after pouring the tea, Lady Violet would regale us all with stories about her home in England, the Bryants' early struggles in America, and the monumental problems she faced daily as supervisor of the meals.

Again and again she explained how, in the beginning, she had tried desperately to anglicize the gastronomical potpourri, but the fact that almost every year brought a new cook of different nationality added to her dilemma. Then, of course, when Josie joined the troupe (and she would give Mother a pained smile) with her Irish recipes, she said that she had accepted total defeat and become resigned to overseeing a kitchen which was, as she put it, "a floating fiasco, fit hoan-ly for the League o' N-eye-tions!"

My grandmother was born at Weston Super Mayor, in England, near Bath, on a date deliberately lost in time. She was christened Violet Nell Chapman, and she told me that the first thing she could remember doing was singing and dressing her one doll in make-believe costumes to be worn on a make-believe stage in a make-believe theater.

At a surprisingly early age, Nellie, as she was called, developed a pleasant soprano voice and quite a mature figure. One night she left her family, her home, and the despised name of Nellie to run away and join a Gilbert and Sullivan company that was touring the provinces.

After an apprenticeship of singing in the chorus, Violet Chapman was given a principal role in *Pinafore* and each night thereafter, she sang, to a delighted audience,

> I'm called Little Buttercup
> Dear Little Buttercup,
> 'Though I could never tell why.
> But, still I'm called Buttercup,
> Poor Little Buttercup,
> Sweet Little Buttercup, I!

It seems only fitting that, a few weeks later, at Bristol, young Samuel Bryant, on his way to a flower show, should accidently bump into "Buttercup," knocking a basket of watercress from her hands.

During the ensuing apologies, explanations, and introductions, Cupid did a first-rate job on Sam, and that evening found him in a shilling stall, listening to *Pinafore* and thrilling to the beauty and sweet voice of Violet Chapman.

After that night, Sam began to follow the company from town to town, traveling over unpaved roads on a high-wheeled velocipede with hard, rubber tires. His courtship, though bumpy and painful, was effective, and within a mercifully few short weeks Violet and Sam were married.

By turning practically everything they owned into cash, the newlyweds managed to purchase two steerage passages aboard a ship bound for America. Violet kept her guitar and a small diamond ring her grandmother had given her, and Sam had his set of carpenter's tools.

It was 1884 when they landed penniless in New York and, on the advice of the Castle Garden authorities, made their way across the bridge to Brooklyn to seek employment. After finding lodging in a rooming house, Violet went to work as a waitress in a restaurant. Sam got a job driving a mule-drawn streetcar from the Brooklyn Bridge to the car barns. They stayed in Brooklyn long enough to have their first child, whom they christened William Edward Bryant. Then, one day, soon after the birth of the baby, Sam had an accident that prompted them to move on.

He was driving the mule car late one afternoon when the sky began to fill with clouds. Low rumbles of thunder worried the beast, and he laid back his ears and shook his head. Suddenly the full force of the storm struck, and a bolt of lightening zigzagged across the dark sky to strike a tree with an ear-splitting crack. It crashed across the tracks directly behind the car, and the mule bolted.

As they rounded a corner, the car tipped over. Sam was thrown in front of it, and the mule broke loose. Belly to the ground and hoofs flailing at the cobblestones, the mule was soon out of sight over the hill. Upon taking inventory, Sam found he had lost a finger, and he immediately decided he wanted nothing more to do with street cars. Violet was sympathetic, and, as they had managed to save a few dollars, they moved to Philadelphia where Sam got a job with a florist. Within a year, a baby girl was born. They named her Florence.

Violet had never really abandoned her plans for a theatrical career, and now, standing beside her husband with little Billy in her arms, and the new infant sleeping in the trunk, in her mind, she was seeing bright lights spelling out "The Four Bryants" on a theater marquee.

Each night, when Sam came home from work, she brought out her guitar. While strumming it softly she would talk about the theater with its glamour and gaiety. Occasionally, she would toss her curls and sing one of Sam's favorite waltzes from the variety halls of London,

> The boys in the gallery for mine,
> The rest of the house may be fine,
> But, they'll stand a fair act and
>   let it down soft,
> Not for the jury box up in the loft.
> Any act they don't think right in line,
> They'll quickly invite to resign.
> You've got to give proof
> To those chaps near the roof,
> The boys in the gallery for mine!

Violet's gentle hints continued to grow more explicit. When they began to border on nagging, Sam capitulated. Using the money he had saved from his job at the florists, he moved the family from Philadelphia to New York and settled them in a boardinghouse. Then, with a command to all of them to stay in the room till he got back, he took his hat and stormed out.

He was gone for a long time, but eventually they heard him calling from the street. Violet ran to the window and looked out. Standing on the curb, holding to the bridle of a huge horse, was Sam. Behind the horse was a wagon, loaded with canvas, poles, boxes, and bottles.

It looked like an ice wagon, but on each side was a giant picture of a swarthy man wearing a turban and staring at a hooded cobra. Beneath the picture in huge letters were the words "Doctor Bryant's Magic Elixir."

"Come on down!" Sam yelled. Violet scooped up the two little ones and rushed downstairs and stood in silence. Finally she asked, "What is it?" and Sam replied, "It's your bloody show business. Pack the grips! We're going west!"

There might have been a discrepancy between Violet's and Sam's idea of show business, but if so, Violet never mentioned it. I guess she felt that a "medicine show" was better than no show at all and, "hafter all," as she said many times, "heverybody 'as to start someplace!"

She was packed and ready to go before you could say, "Which way to the opera house?" Tucking Billy and Florence inside the wagon, she climbed to the driver's seat and sat beside her husband as they drove out of town, smiling and waving at every passerby.

At the edge of town, as the cobblestone street gave way to a dusty road, startled birds fluttered from the trees as a clear soprano voice informed them,

> I'm called Little Buttercup . . .
> Poor Little Buttercup,
> Sweet Little Buttercup, I!

Violet Bryant had definitely returned to the profession, but it would be quite some time before she found her true place in it, as the queenly matriarch of a famous Floating Theater.

THE FOUR BRYANTS

According to Violet's recollections, when the family left New York in the medicine show wagon, none of them realized they were starting a trip of several years which would take them as far west as New Mexico.

During that time they would do a "high pitch" in the small towns, with Violet drawing a crowd by playing her guitar and singing. Then Sam would mystify them with a few feats of very bad magic. His best and most reliable trick was called a "sucker box." It consisted of a small, black wooden box with two hinged doors in one side. The object was to make an oversized dice disappear into its innards. Sam told me himself that it was practically impossible to *keep* the dice from disappearing and he should have been billed as "the world's worst magician!"

Nevertheless, Violet was delighted. Sam was finally in show business. When the crowd became large enough, he would go into his pitch which promised near miraculous cures of soreness, lameness, neuralgia, rheumatism, gout, shingles, stiffness, congestion, and pain. All the while, he would be holding up the bottle with its colorful label that warned, "Keep away from fire!"—a wise precaution since the sole ingredients of the elixir were gasoline and red pepper. Dad told me the gasoline opened the pores and the red pepper made them forget anything that hurt. Then, shaking his head, he'd add, "Thank goodness they rubbed it on. They didn't drink it!"

The Four Bryants—Billy, Florence, Violet, and Sam—in their Medicine Show days

When they came to a larger town, they would stay two days. On the first day they would do a high pitch, and on the second day they would put up the tent and charge ten cents to see a show.

During their trek the Bryants crossed and recrossed Pennsylvania, Ohio, Indiana, Illinois, Missouri, Texas, New Mexico, and Colorado. In April of 1898 they found themselves crossing the border onto the strip of Indian territory that would in a few years become Oklahoma. On April 22, they took part in the land run across the Cherokee Strip. They staked out a claim but lost it to some bunko artists who swindled hundreds of people out of their land by claiming to be government surveyors. So the Bryants moved on. At one point during their travels they were doing well and decided to enlarge the show. To that end, they hired Frank L. Cutler with his daughter, Myra, and a comedian named Joe Keaton. Eventually Myra married Joe, and they became the parents of a baby boy who was to become the famous Buster Keaton of silent movies.

Dad always shook his head when he described what he called their "fluctuating fortunes" that went constantly from bad to good to bad to good and then back to bad again. He told me they reached an all-time low in Raton, New Mexico, a few miles from the Colorado border. Just as they were thinking that there was nothing left to go wrong, Sam was arrested for peddling without a license, and the horse, wagon, and tent were confiscated in lieu of a fine.

Typically refusing to acknowledge a setback, much less defeat, Violet pointed out that, as the horse and wagon were gone anyway, it might be an auspicious time for them to break into what she referred to as "legitimate theater."

They managed to make their way to Kansas City, and during their haphazard journey they put together their act, a collection of songs, dances, and funny sayings. Almost immediately after they arrived, they secured an engagement at the opera house. "The Four Bryants," as they billed themselves, had begun their precarious vaudeville career.

When they closed in Kansas City they began barnstorming their way east. They arrived in Buffalo, New York, in the middle of the winter of 1900. The only work they could find was in a concert hall known as Bonney's Comique on Canal Street.

Concert halls were forerunners of the beer halls of the twentieth century and were constructed with drinking more than entertainment in mind. The audiences were loud, coarse, and vulgar, and it was with a collective sigh of almost relief that the Bryants, through no fault of their own, lost their job there. It was late in February when Mrs. Bonney nailed a sign to her door. It read, "Closed for repair."

Violet immediately bought a copy of the *Clipper*, a theatrical trade paper of the day. Then she led her brood to the boardinghouse and settled them around Sam, who sat close to the lamp to scan the want ads. After reading aloud several advertisements that inspired moans and groans from his audience, he suddenly said, "How does this sound?" and read, "Wanted for Captain Price's Water Queen Showboat Vaudeville people in all lines. Long, pleasant engagement."

Dad told me none of them had even heard of a showboat until then but they liked the sound of "Long, pleasant engagement." Violet wrote to Captain Price, and a few days later they received a telegram. "All O.K. Join at Augusta, Kentucky, Saturday." It took a lot of wheeling and dealing to collect the railroad fare, but they managed and, with a grip in each hand and a property trunk in the baggage coach ahead, the Four Bryants boarded a train for the Ohio River.

At Augusta, Kentucky, they stepped onto the station platform and into a different world. They made their way to the landing and found the *Water Queen*. It was the first showboat the Bryants had ever seen. She was beautiful with her fresh white paint, lacy gingerbread work running around the top, and huge circles of delicately carved wood decorating the second deck.

It was, for all of them, a case of love at first sight. The Bryants had found their true home, and the river audiences responded to their enthusiasm with wild acclaim. Even Sam's less-than-good magic was a huge success.

Captain Price, one of the most colorful and well-known showboat captains, proved to be a kind, understanding, and generous man, and when their very successful season ended at New Orleans he magnanimously paid their fare back to Cincinnati. But, if he thought it would end there, he was sadly mistaken.

Within a few, short years the barns, outbuildings, and fences along the rivers would be papered with colorful showbills announcing:

Bryant's Showboat
presenting
A Girl of the Under World
With Vaudeville
Between Acts
Let's All Go!

But, for the time being, the Bryants were again "at liberty." They bought a span of mules, a wagon, and a supply of gasoline and red pepper. Their plan was to high pitch their way to Pittsburgh, but their hearts weren't in it. They talked constantly and fondly of their wonderful summer on board the *Water Queen*, and in spite of Sam's snort of derision at the idea, Violet spoke openly and often of her newfound dream to own a showboat.

By the time they got to Pittsburgh it was early spring, and they turned the mules up the Allegheny River to the little town of West Hickory, Pennsylvania, where the principal industry was the construction of wooden barges.

They took lodging in a rooming house. The next morning Sam was up with the sun. He strolled down to the riverbank, which was lined with barges under construction. He was gone all day but reappeared at suppertime to declare, rather defiantly, that he was going to build a boat.

To everyone's surprise the work of a shipwright came easily to Sam. He had only the few tools he had brought from England, but with them he was able to construct a serviceable flatboat ten feet wide and thirty feet long. It was just large enough to hold the Four Bryants, the mules, and the wagon.

They pushed off from shore and soon found themselves in midstream, rushing down the river with practically no means of control. Dad said they hit the bank first on one side of the river and then on the other. At New Kensington, Pennsylvania, they scraped a bridge pier, and one night the boat ran up on an island with such force one of the mules fell overboard.

Eventually they reached that point where the Allegheny and the Monongahela rivers merge. As they drifted onto the beautiful Ohio, they were pleased to find that it was more placid and had a much slower current than the Allegheny. As they made their way downstream, summer, like the river, glided by. At a point four miles below Gallipolis, they got stuck on a sandbar for over a week. There and then they decided to tie up for the winter. They had a towboat pull them up to Neal's Run Creek, near the mouth of the Little Kanawha. There they settled in for what proved to be a severe winter, and in February,

Sam
Bryant

when the ice broke, their little boat was destroyed. However, it happened too late, for they had already been captivated by the magic of the river.

Dad said the next thing Sam built was a little towboat they named the *Florence*. Then they bought a little houseboat which they had until 1906, when a large raft of railroad ties brushed against them and sank the whole outfit. At nearby Point Pleasant, West Virginia, the citizens rushed forward to help, and the banker there found them a 16 x 90 foot barge which they bought for twenty-five dollars. They raised the *Florence* and cleaned her up. Then Dad and Sam went to work building their first real showboat.

By spring of 1907 they were ready with the *Princess*, a little Floating Theater that seated 140 people. With tickets at fifteen, twenty, and thirty-five cents, they opened at Point Pleasant to standing room only. The auditorium was filled, and the guards were crowded with wonderfully generous people who had taken a personal interest in the career of the Four Bryants.

They toured with the *Princess* for ten years. In 1915, they needed a piano player who could also play the calliope they had just acquired. They placed an ad in the *Billboard* and in response received a telegram from one Joe Costello. It read, "At Liberty. Experienced Pianist. Salary your limit. Can join at once without ticket." Dad told me that Violet said, "Joe Costello. 'e must be Hitalian. Hitalians are very musical. Let's 'ire 'im." Under the assumption that they were engaging an Italian man, they wired confirmation to Joe Costello. When the pianist arrived, they were astounded to find they had hired a lovely young Irish colleen named Josephine "Cos-low."

It was their last season on the *Princess*. The following year, they sold the entire outfit and proceeded to build the *Bryant's New Showboat*. When it was finished, they purchased the steamboat *Valley Belle*.

Josephine Costello married Billy Bryant at the end of 1916, thus setting the stage for my appearance some six years later.

THE PLAY! THE PLAY!

Until the end of the nineteenth century, showboat programs consisted mainly of vaudeville offerings which included singers, dancers, comics, and novelty acts. Occasionally, a short sketch would be added, but the pattern of a three-act drama with specialties instead of intermissions was not established until 1900 when E.E. Eisenbarth, at the insistence of his wife, presented two plays on board the *Modern Temple of Amusement*.

The new policy proved to be such a success that by the end of the year most of the showboats were presenting full-length plays. Sometimes scripts were purchased but more often they were borrowed and copied by hand. Others came from performers. An actor applying for work might write: "Have complete wardrobe for drawing room, western, Rube and Tom. Also have scripts for *The Plunger*, *A Builder of Bridges*, and *Girl of the Golden West*."

The scripts were usually written on legal size paper, bound in oilcloth with the rough side out and with the title printed in bold letters on the front of the cover.

Most scripts called for a cast of five men and three women. The male parts consisted of a heavy, or villain, a juvenile lead, a comic, a character man, and "General Business," a heading that covered such parts as partner to the villain, pal to the lead, or brother to the heroine. The women's parts were leads, ingenues, a soubrette who played opposite the comic, a villainess, and sometimes a character woman. Anything beyond these limits was handled by doubling. That is, one actor doing one part in the first act, then donning a wig and mustache for another character in the second act, and sometimes another in the last act as well.

The plays were extremely moral. Good was good and bad was bad and there were no gray areas. The leading man, after being falsely accused of murder, might temporarily drop from sight at the end of the first act, but he would invariably return with proof of his innocence in time for the final curtain.

In the true spirit of the old ballad "She's More to Be Pitied Than Censured," good women were allowed to fall, even so far as to produce an illegitimate child, but only in supporting roles.

The heroine was often forced to struggle through the bulk of the play, seemingly under a cloud of guilt, but she must eventually be proven pure as the driven snow. Periodically, she would face her accusers and the audience and deliver lines such as,

"I'd rather DIE than say 'yes'!"

"You would not say that, sir, if JACK were only here!"

"If this be aristocracy, thank GOD I'm a country girl!" and my favorite,

"Rags are royal raiment when worn for virtue's sake!"

Villains were either city bankers who wore mustaches and carried mortgages or unshaven, brutish clods with uncombed hair and heavy eyebrows.

The leading man was either a parson or a country boy with a slow drawl and broad shoulders bulging under a blue flannel shirt worn open at the throat. Known to actors as a "blue shirt lead," he would, at the drop of a villain's sneer, flex his pectoral muscles, draw himself up to his full height, and say, "Sir, you are speaking of the woman I love!"

Each script had a cast list with a few words of description on the character, as in my favorite play, *Tess of the Storm Country*.

Tess of the Storm Country
Cast of Characters

Tessible Skinner .... Ingenue lead
Teola Graves .... Emotional woman
Nancy Longman .... Squatter woman.
                           Mender of nets.
Fredrick Graves .... Preacher lead
Ben Letts .... Heavy. Fisherman.
Oran Skinner .... Tessible's father
Elias Graves .... Politician
Ezra Longman .... Low Comedy
Tom Hecker .... Game warden

The plot centers around Tessible Skinner and involves three families. Tess and her father, Oran Skinner, live in a shack by the river. Each night Skinner goes out with the other squatters to net fish illegally for a living. Elias Graves is a powerful politician who lives with his son and daughter. The son is a preacher who, in his work with the squatters, meets and falls in love with Tess. His sister is Teola, the "emotional woman" who falls in love with the game warden and secretly bears his child.

During the first act, the squatters are surprised by the game warden. Ben Letts kills the warden but manages to place the blame on Tess's father. Ezra, the comic, played by Dad, is a witness to the murder, but Ben hits him over the head, and, for the next two acts, Ezra wanders in and out of the play in a hopeless daze. Tess's father is taken to jail, and she is left alone in the cabin.

When the second act opens, four months have passed. Tess is alone in the cabin. Teola Graves staggers in out of the snow with her newborn baby. When she threatens suicide, Tess offers to keep the child for her. Teola returns to her home, promising to leave milk out for Tess to "steal." Ben Letts appears on the scene and tries to force himself upon Tess. Because she scorns him, he tells the entire community the baby in the cabin is hers.

The next morning, while "stealing" milk from the Graves

house, Tess is apprehended by Elias Graves, who takes a whip to her. The baby becomes ill, and, fearful that it may die without being baptised, Tess takes it to Parson Fred Graves, the man she loves.

The last act is in the little mission church. Ezra recovers his wits and clears Tess's father. Nancy finds out it was Ben Letts who wronged her daughter Mary and is delighted to hear he is going to be arrested.

Teola tells everyone the baby Tess has been caring for is hers. (Teola is forgiven because she is not the heroine.) Tess is vindicated, and Frederick asks her to be his wife. Justice triumphs as Ben Letts is led away to prison and Tess's father is freed.

In the final scene, everyone on stage crowds into the pews and Frederick opens a book of hymns. "Hymn number 220," he announces, and everyone sings:

Mine eyes have seen the glory
Of the coming of the Lord.
He is trampling out the vintage
Where the grapes of wrath are stored.
He hath loosed the fateful lightning
Of His terrible swift sword.
His truth is marching on.

During this song, Dad (as Ezra) would pick up a broomstick, to which a cigar box had been affixed at one end, and take up a collection, according to the direction in the script:

(Ezra passes collection box. First three people put in money. Comes to Tom Hecker who keeps singing and ignores prodding. Ezra hits him on top of head with box. Tom puts in money. Goes on to sheriff who shows his badge. Finishes the collection. Stops stage right, behind singers. Dumps coins from box into his hand. Counts money and pockets same as curtain slowly descends with cast singing)

Glory, glory, hallelujah!
Glory, glory, hallelujah!
Glory, glory, hallelujah!
His truth is marching on!

THE ACTORS
HAVE ARRIVED

Most of the showboats tied up for three months during the winter at various protective landings. Point Pleasant, West Virginia, was a favorite spot, as was Paducah, Kentucky. Until 1931, we wintered at West Elizabeth, Pennsylvania, and then moved to Point Pleasant.

In November, at the end of the season, the actors would bid us a reluctant farewell with promises to return in the spring. They would go by train to various towns or cities to join stock companies or tab shows. The crew would stay on board long enough to take the boats to winter quarters and then they too would go their separate ways. The family would stay a few weeks and then head for New York or Chicago. Only a watchman remained on board. After a sabbatical of three months, the members of the steamboat crew, last to leave in the fall, were the first to come aboard in the spring. Scrub and paint brushes were brought out, decks were caulked and the roof freshly tarred. Then the actors began to arrive.

They would scramble down the riverbank a week before the opening, waving and shouting. After exchanging greetings with everyone on board they'd head for the steamboat to select their staterooms and unpack. Then, they would gather in the galley to drink the strong, hot coffee that was always available and to talk excitedly of the season ahead.

We carried, besides the family, a leading man, a villain, a juve-

A visiting relative learning to use the draw bucket

nile, a character man, and occasionally a man and wife general business team. Single actors lived on the *Valley Belle* in tiny staterooms. Each room was furnished with a bunk, a washstand, and a mirror. On top of the washstand sat a pitcher and bowl and beneath it was a bucket with a long rope attached to the handle. This "draw bucket" could be thrown over the side and brought up filled with cool, clear and, at that time, unpolluted water for washing. A coal oil lamp was bracketed to one wall, for while a generator furnished electricity for the evening's performance, it was turned off after the show.

By today's standards, their accommodations were practically

primitive, but the actors were a happy lot. Compared to their lives on shore a showboat season had much to offer. While their contemporaries on land struggled on and off trains carrying props, scenery, and baggage, made sleeper jumps while sitting up in a day coach, and did two to ten shows a day in damp, dirty theaters, showboat performers, by comparison, lived the life of Riley. With no thought to packing or catching a train, they ate, slept, and traveled on board, gliding dreamlike between willow-lined shores to wake each day in a different town, with their theater a stone's throw from their sleeping quarters.

An actor on the road lived with the ever-present fear of finding himself stranded a thousand miles from nowhere as the result of a show being canceled or an unscrupulous manager absconding with the funds. The showboat actor gloried in the guarantee of a full "play or pay" season, secure in the knowledge that his salary would be waiting in the box office each Saturday with the regularity of a Swiss watch.

Fifteen dollars a week sounds ludicrous, but with no agents' fees to pay, no traveling or living expenses, in fact, no place to spend money if you wanted to, it was not unusual for an actor at the end of a season to head home with six hundred dollars in his grouch bag, or twelve hundred for a man and wife team. The overland thespian who received much more than that per week rarely found it possible to save anything near that amount.

In addition, the showboat actor enjoyed a minimum of labor and a maximum of love from his adoring fans. One performance a night, never on Sunday and no matinees, a week's rehearsal in the spring, another in the summer, and the rest of the time was his own.

Afternoons were often spent strolling through the village where they were warmly greeted by the friendly farmers and their families. Other long, lazy days were filled with writing letters and reading. Some went exploring and others swam, but it was a rare actor who didn't take advantage of the ever-present privilege of casting a fish

Josephine, on the
Illinois River

line off the fantail of the steamboat, over the protective guardrail that
ran the full length of the outside of the showboat, or even from the
end of a long, cane pole, right out through the door of his stateroom.

While each spring brought letters from numerous actors who
were anxious to work on a showboat, we seldom had more than one
or two new cast members a season. The regulars returned year after
year, bringing with them personal touches for their rooms: a bedspread, a hand-painted pillow, and tiny alcohol stoves to heat tea or
soup for their "night lunch" after the show. While vaudeville performers and actors in legitimate theater spoke of having "supper"

after the last show, people in tent shows or on showboats always referred to that late night snack as "night lunch." Whether a bowl of soup, a sandwich, crackers and cheese or a complete meal, it was "night lunch."

On the first day or two of the season, if you walked down the hallway flanked by the staterooms you would hear whistling, singing, humming, and hammering as happy actors drove countless nails into the walls to hang pictures, souvenir programs, newspaper clippings, perhaps a what-not shelf, and usually some sort of good luck talisman, for most actors were incurably superstitious.

Besides the customary need to avoid black cats, spilled salt, the number thirteen, and leaning ladders, actors also had a slew of occupational taboos that ranged from not whistling in the dressing room to not putting your dancing shoes on the makeup table.

Peacock feathers were frowned on, and the color yellow was never to be worn on stage. Discovering a hat on the bed was almost as bad as finding a bird flying in the auditorium. An actor would rather be caught whistling "Home Sweet Home" (a dire omen) than quoting from Shakespeare's *Macbeth*, and to say the curtain line (the last line of the play) at rehearsal was to risk not only the wrath of the Fates but a tongue-lashing from the other members of the cast as well.

At supper the first evening of the new season, the dining room would overflow with noisy chatter as old friends exchanged tales of the triumphs or tragedies of their winter tours and regaled newcomers with stories of past seasons on the showboat. Sometimes an old-timer would take it upon himself to explain the few but stringent rules of life on board the *Bryant's Showboat*. There was no gambling, drinking, or smoking allowed, and members of the opposite sex were not to be entertained on board. On the rare occasions when we hired an unmarried lady, she lived on the showboat proper with the family, and while fraternization with the male members of the troupe was not strictly forbidden, it certainly wasn't encouraged. Everyone sat drinking coffee long after the tables had been cleared, talking and laughing and reveling in their anticipation for the tour ahead.

Finally, they would settle down, return to their staterooms and prepare for bed. Exhausted from their long journeys and emotionally drained, they would climb gratefully into their bunks. The gentle swaying of the boat and the sound of waves slapping softly against the side lulled them to sleep immediately.

The next day, after an early breakfast, the entire cast would make their way to the front end of the showboat and up the stairs to my grandparents' quarters. They would pay their respects to Sam and Lady Violet and then, at Violet's invitation, arrange themselves comfortably in chairs around the room. Soon the rest of the family would arrive—Mother, myself, and Dad with the script and the parts.

Unlike today's theatrical productions in which each member of the cast has a copy of the play, only the director had a complete script. The actors' roles were written on half sheets of typing paper called "sides." They contained only the actor's lines and the last few words of the preceding line, to be used as a cue. These sides were then covered with oilcloth, like the script, and bound together with brads or stitches. For example:

COVER PAGE:

TEN NIGHTS IN A BARROOM
part of
SAMPLE SWICHEL

SAMPLE SHEET:
ACT THREE. SCENE ONE.
(ENTER R) Well, things have certainly changed around here in the past ten years. I've knocked off the rum and it's about time I settled down and got married. Here comes Mehitable Cartright. I might as well ask her.
——— (MEHIT ENTERS) looking all over for you!
Well, I've been looking for you. I want to ask you something.
——— what is it Sample?
Well, I haven't had a drink in over a year and I've got a job. I think it's about

time you and me got married. That is, if you'll have me.
———— this is so sudden.
Sudden? Sudden? I've been going with that girl nigh onto twenty years and
she says it's sudden. Well, if you don't want me, I'll go down to Sam Walk-
er's house and ask his cook. She'll have me.
———— didn't say I wouldn't have you.
Then you will? (BUS) How about a kiss to seal the bargain? Pucker up.
(BUS) Sweet cider, right out of the bung hole!

On the back of each sheet, or side, the actor would write the cues
without his lines in order to facilitate studying his part.

Dad wore many hats, among them that of a director. Before
casting, he would talk with the actors about their other theatrical
talents. Almost everyone could double in brass (play a musical instrument) and/or perform at least one vaudeville-type routine.

According to the actors' capabilities and the flexibility of the
parts they were to play, Dad would line up the show. Perhaps a
singer and a juggler would perform between the first and second
acts and a magician and a comic would precede the prize candy sale
between the second and third acts.

Then Dad would announce the show we were opening with
and distribute the parts, calling out the names of the characters as
he handed them out.

"We're doing *Ten Nights in a Barroom* on the way downriver.
Clyde, you do Harvey Green. You've played it before. Gordon, Willie
Hammond. Carlton, Joe Morgan. We're doing the cut version." Per-
haps, when he said, "Milton, you're playing Frank Slade," Milton
might ask, "How many sides?" or an actor might interrupt to boast,
"I did Archibald in *East Lynne* last winter with Carrie Cruthers.
Forty-seven sides!" And so it went until all the parts were assigned.

Then everyone would settle in and the first, or "reading," rehearsal would start. We would read through the whole play with
Dad, as director, stopping at any place marked (BUS)—for stage
business—to explain what it meant, according to the master script,
or Dad's inventive mind. The actor involved would pencil it in on

his part. At times Dad would say, "Milton, on this scene, you're off [stage], so dim the lights for Mary's exit and then bring them up again for the fight," or "Gordon, Josie's on stage in this scene so you play the piano for it. 'Hearts and Flowers' all the way through."

When the rehearsal was over, there would be a brief discussion about wardrobe to find out who had what and how much had to be supplemented or made. By then, the bell was ringing for lunch and everyone would thank Sam and Lady Violet, make a hasty exit, and scurry around the guard to the steamboat, a horde of hungry actors. In the afternoon, some of them brought out the sheet music for their specialties and ran through them with Mother at the piano. The others retired to their staterooms to do some serious wood-shedding on their roles.

They had exactly six days in which to complete six rehearsals, learn their lines, perfect their specialties, arrange for their wardrobe, and be standing in the wings on opening night, waiting for their cue to enter.

They always made it!

WILLIE

I can honestly say that as a child on the showboat I never met an actor I didn't like. They were all very patient with me and extremely supportive of my young career. They were never too busy to answer my questions and would spend hours teaching me their specialties. Of course, I learned dancing, acting, and directing from Dad, but a long line of thespian tutors contributed generously to my theatrical education.

Besides those who introduced me to slack-wire walking, hoop rolling, and the wonderful world of magic, I remember fondly Vic Faust, who taught me how to play a one-stringed fiddle, Gordon Ray, who showed me how to tap dance on roller skates, and Carl Adamson, who instructed me in the fascinating art of chalk talk.

Carl was an old-timer, probably in his early sixties. In the plays he did character parts, grandfathers, sages, old prospectors, and such. But for his specialty between the acts, he did chalk talk and paper tearing.

He worked with big chunks of colored chalk and a large drawing board. About fifteen or twenty equally large sheets of blank white paper were bolted at each corner to the board. In the center of the back of the board was a bolt that went through the top of the easel and was secured by a large, adjustable wing nut. This allowed the board *and* the drawing to be turned sideways or upside down.

Carl would enter wearing a beret and a large, black artist's smock over his costume for the play. He would set the easel center stage, then go back and bring out a tiny table which held the chalk. He would smile and say, "Good evening, ladies and gentlemen. My, what a fine-looking group we have here tonight. I am going to perform for you a demonstration of the ancient and honorable art of chalk painting, but I want to tell you in advance what my dear old mother once told to me. 'As you go through life, believe nothing of what you hear and only half of what you see.' Allow me to show you what I mean."

With that, he would turn his back on the audience and face the drawing board, completely blocking their view. Mother, at the piano, would play "Turkey in the Straw" over and over until Carl turned back to the audience, revealing a primitive sketch of a cow.

Carl would ask the audience, "What do you see?"
Everyone would shout, "A COW!"
"Are you sure?" Carl would tease.
"YES!" they would scream.
"That's strange. I see Farmer Brown!"
Mother would play "The Farmer in the Dell" and Carl would turn back to the drawing board to make a few quick strokes on the original. Again he would face the audience and say, pointing to the altered picture, "Do you STILL see a cow?"

The audience would stare and a few would giggle, but some die-hard would always shout, "YES!!"

Then, turning the board and picture upside down, Carl would ask,

"WHAT ABOUT NOW?" A Tah-Tah! from Mother on the piano and the audience would go wild.

On the wave of their applause, Carl would rip the sheet off the board, walk to the side of the stage and give the picture to someone in the audience. Then he would begin to speak again. As he talked, he drew.

"I am sure you know, ladies and gentlemen, that many, many people all over the world are superstitious. In fact, how many of you out there tonight knocks on wood, throws spilled salt over your left shoulder, or carries a rabbit's foot in your pocket or purse?" He would turn to face them with a warm and knowing smile. Then back to the board with, "It's a known fact, that a baseball player often carries a horseshoe in his pocket for good luck."

He would turn and step aside to reveal the picture of a horseshoe that he had drawn. Then he would say, "Well, now. We seem to have the horseshoe, but no ball player." Then to mother, "If you please."

Mother would break into a rousing chorus of "Take Me Out to the Ball Game" while Carl made bold, swift strokes with his chalk. As the song came to an end, he would turn, step aside, and bow to another round of applause.

After again giving the picture away, he would return to center stage and ask for someone to tell him his or her name.

Everyone would scream at once: Bob! Tom! Catherine! Clyde! Pearl! Nellie! Such bedlam allowed him to choose any name he wanted, for no one could tell whether or not it had been called.

He had a half a dozen practiced sketches, and it was a rare audience in those days that didn't contain at least one Helen, Rose, Ruth, Mary, Kate, or Beth. Mary seemed to be his favorite and he would always choose a girl with that name if possible. He would then draw, on the board:

He would bow to Mother. She would start to play, and sing in her sweet Irish voice, "Mary is a Grand Old Name." Carl would draw.

> For it was "Mary, Mary"
> Plain as any name can be,
> But with propriety, society
> Will say, "Marie."
> But it was "Mary, Mary"
> Long before the fashions came

At this point she would look at Carl to see how far along he was, then she would time her dramatic pauses accordingly.

> And there is something there!
> (Pause)
> That sounds so square,
> It's a grand,
> (Pause)
> Old
> (Pause)
> Name.

Carl would step back with a flourish of his hand like one of the old masters, presenting the portrait.

Then, to a continuous round of applause, he would carefully tear the sheet from the board, wave the original to the side of the stage, hand it to her over the footlights, and kiss her hand. On more than one occasion, I thought the girl was going to swoon.

Carl would bow, leave the stage to allow the applause to build, and then return with a sheet of colored tissue paper, six feet long and one foot wide. He would smile and fold the paper, fanlike, ending with a 1 x 1 foot square.

Then, as Mother sang and played "Put Them All Together They Spell Mother," he would swiftly and spastically rip little bits and pieces out of the folded tissue paper. At the end of the song, as Mother shouted the words against her own dynamic chords, "A word that means the world . . . to me!" Carl would unfold the tissue paper to reveal a six-foot-long set of joined letters that spelled M O T H E R!

There wouldn't be a dry eye in the house!

Gordon Ray was with us for several seasons. He was also a general business actor but younger than Carl. He played convicts, soldiers, second heavies, and occasionally, friend of the leading man. As a specialty, Gordon played the accordion, sometimes while wearing roller skates, and he did a comedy routine which, in various versions, was popular with both audiences and entertainers. It was called "A Letter From Home."

Gordon would come on wearing baggy pants, a plaid shirt, and a porkpie hat. He would grin at the audience and say, "Hello out there. I just come from the post office and I got a letter from home. I haven't read it yet. But I thought maybe you folks would like to hear it too." He would take an envelope from his pocket, open it, and take out a handwritten letter of two or three pages. Then he read.

> September, October, No Wonder, 1900 and
> Froze to death.

My dear, darling, orphan son.

[To the audience] Orphan. My paw's outta work again. Every time my paw gets out of work, my ma calls me orphan.

[reads] My dear, darling, orphan son,

I thought I would write you these few lines to let you know how we all are. We are all well. Your sister is sick. She ate some green apples and got the tummy ache. Your pa went to give her some medicine and by mistake gave her carbolic acid. Now, they've arrested yer pa for puttin' acid inside her [in cider].

Minnie Hinklebottom got a new bicycle last week. She was riding it down the steep hill back of the old red barn when she ran into a barbed-wire fence. It bruised her [looks closely at paper] somewhat and hurt her [turns the page] otherwise.

Last week, your brother went hunting and treed a rabbit. We had to lock him in the woodshed and feed him his meals on the end of a long pole. If the wind is in the right direction, we will let him out next Saturday.

We are building a new brick house. We are taking the bricks out of the old brick house and putting them into the new brick house. We are living in the old brick house until the new brick house is finished.

We have six new hens and a new minister. The hens lay eggs every day. The minister is going to lay a [turns page] cornerstone down at the church next Sunday.

I am sending you your winter coat as you asked me to. It was too heavy to go by parcel post so I cut off the buttons. You will find them in the right-hand pocket.

Your loving mother.

P.S. [to audience] My ma always writes a P.S. [reads] P.S. I was going to send you ten dollars in this letter but I had the envelope all sealed up.

There was only one actor who ever hurt me, and though, in retrospect, I realize that he didn't do it intentionally, he did break my five-year-old heart.

I can't even remember his name. It was his partner Willie that I was in love with. Willie had a mop of red hair and a freckled face dominated by huge blue eyes that he rolled from side to side.

Willie was a ventriloquist's dummy, but I absolutely refused to believe that he was anything less than a young Tom Swift. Each time he was about to perform, I would rush to the orchestra pit and sit next to mother on the piano bench, gazing adoringly at my idol. At the finish of his act, Willie always sang a song entitled "I Get the Blues When it Rains," and one night the ventriloquist decided to add a new piece of business to the number.

Through the use of a concealed hose, running from Willie's eyes, down through his wooden innards to a bulb in the vent's hand, he planned to have the dummy spray a light shower of water into the air at the end of the song.

Unaware of the torch I was carrying, no one bothered to inform me of the change. That night I was sitting, as usual, in the pit, hanging on Willie's every borrowed word. Each time the audience laughed at one of his jokes, I clapped my hands and squirmed and squealed. Finally, he rolled his eyes and nodded to my mother to begin to play. She gave him a rippling arpeggio, and Willie began to croon in his nasal tones.

> I get the blues when it rains
> The blues I can't lose when it rains
> Each little drop that falls
> On my window pane
> Seems to remind me
> Of the tears I shed in vain.
> I sit and wait for the sun
> To shine down on me once again.
> It rained when I found you,
> It rained when I lost you,
> That's why I get the blues when it rains.

I sighed as Willie seemed to smile in my direction, but then, suddenly, he began to spray! Right on me!

The ventriloquist had misjudged the distance, and I was in the direct line of fire. As the water hit me, I began to scream and I tore out of the pit, under the stage, and up the ladder, feeling like the leading lady in *Tilly's Punctured Romance*.

My father found me in the greenroom, curled up in the bottom of a steamer trunk, my inevitable refuge in time of disaster. When he gathered me in his arms and asked why I was crying, I couldn't find words to explain the pain of a five-year-old broken heart.

The best I could manage, between sobs, was, "WILLIE . . . SPIT . . . ON . . . ME!"

DEAD MEN
TELL NO TALES

Unlike the actors, cabin boys and deckhands were expendable breeds who seldom stayed for a whole season. They were young, fast-growing farm or shantyboat boys with appetites that prompted Dad to declare, "I'd rather pay 'em than keep 'em."

They usually came on board, ate like a carp, worked for a while, and then left for various reasons. A few succumbed to homesickness, others just drifted off to different jobs, and at least one young man fled for his life.

Our cook that year was a professional chef who dressed the part. He had white shoes, white pants, a white coat, a chef's hat, and a chef's apron. He also had a chef's temperament. His name was Henry, but he pronounced it "On-*ree.*"

Henry's pride and joy was a big, black, iron griddle that covered half the top of the old wood-burning stove. He brought it with him when he joined, carefully wrapped in a piece of oilcloth. He used it exclusively for making pancakes and guarded it like a precious jewel.

Neither butter nor oil touched the surface of that griddle, only a piece of what Henry called "lucky leather." It was a six-inch square of thick bacon rind with a heavy string looped through a hole in one corner. He kept it hanging on a nail inside the icebox and before making pancakes, rubbed it over the black iron from rim to rim until it shone like patent leather.

The griddle was never washed. After each use he would pour salt over the surface and heat it until the salt turned brown. Then he would scrape it off with a wooden spatula and rub the griddle down with a crumpled piece of brown butcher paper. At night, he took it to his stateroom and tucked it under his bed.

One morning after breakfast he had gone out on the fantail to enjoy a cool breeze and he came back just in time to see the cabin boy preparing to dunk the nearly sacred griddle in a tub of sudsy dishwater. Henry's face turned white.

"STOP!" he yelled. Grabbing the startled lad by the collar and pants seat, he danced him out of the kitchen, screaming all the while. "Are you crazy? What do you think you're doing? That's a PANCAKE Griddle. You understand? A PANCAKE GRIDDLE!" As they reached the rail, he heaved his burden over the side, yelling, "I'LL TEACH YOU TO RESPECT THE TOOLS OF THE TRADE!"

The cabin boy swam to shore and climbed out of the water. He shook himself like a dog and turned for a final look at Henry who was still screaming and shaking his fist. Then, he scurried up the bank, over the top, and away. He never returned.

One season we were doing a Civil War play which, in one scene, called for a brief and silent appearance by Abe Lincoln. Our deck-hand was tall and slender and had high hopes of becoming an actor, so Dad assigned him the part.

The young man became so involved with his first role he spent the entire season perfecting his character. He grew a beard, scrounged a tall hat, foulard tie, and shawl from country stores, and kept old envelopes and a pencil stub in his pocket.

In the afternoon, when his chores were done and any sensible deckhand would curl up for a well-earned nap, our hero would change from his overalls into his costume and stroll up the river-bank and into the village, where he created quite a stir.

One day he left the boat, climbed the riverbank and paused at the top. He took out an envelope and made a notation on it. My grandfather was on the front deck with Dad. He watched in silence as the deckhand strolled toward town. Then he turned to Dad and said, "Billy, that boy isn't going to be satisfied until somebody assassinates him!"

The boy I remember best was another beanpole about seventeen years old who looked like a young Henry Fonda. Dad called him "Spar-pole." Born and raised on a farm, he'd never been further from home than the north corner of the south forty, and when the showboat came to town with its cargo of make-believe, he suddenly realized that there was more to life than forkin' fertilizer and sloppin' hogs.

After the show, he lingered on the deck till everyone else had gone ashore. Then, with a burst of bravado, he marched up to Dad and informed him that he wanted to be an actor and he was willing to do anything to learn how. Dad took one look at that handsome profile and immediately signed him on, regaling him with promises to teach him the secrets of the profession.

Spar-pole was by far the most conscientious cabin boy we ever had. Every morning he had the fire in the cookstove lit and the woodbox filled long before the cook had rolled out of bed. No task was too menial or too difficult, and he sailed through the work-filled days, steering by the stars in his eyes.

Besides his regular duties in the galley, he scrubbed decks, hauled coal, painted scenery, swept out the auditorium, and scraped the old chewing gum from under the bottoms of the seats. At night, he would sit in the balcony and run the spotlight, mouthing the words of every line in the show and thrilling vicariously to each burst of laughter or round of applause.

Spar-pole's rather premature departure was motivated by a strange set of circumstances. Sometimes a showboat would head in at a landing where miles and miles of mud stretched in either direction with nothing more substantial to tie to than a beached bull-head, or catfish. On these occasions, the crew would dig a hole about five feet deep. In it they would bury a log with a long chain around its middle. Once the log was buried, the showboat's line could be secured to the free end of the chain, which was left sticking out of the ground. These logs were called "deadmen."

Spar-pole had only been with us a short time when one of the rare incidents of violence on board erupted. The show was over and Spar-pole was standing on the bank at the end of the gangplank, holding a lantern for the people who were leaving.

Suddenly, with a hair-raising rebel yell, a young backwoodsman who had been scorned by his lady love charged down the riverbank, firing a rifle at his hated rival, who was just about to step ashore. Hit, with blood gushing freely from a wound in his shoulder, the young man fell back into the arms of Spar-pole, knocking the lantern to the ground. With an oath, the deckhand dropped the bloody burden and ran for his stateroom where he prudently locked the door and probably hid under the bunk.

The victim was taken home, and the avenged lover disappeared over the hill and into the night. The crowd dispersed, the lights on board were extinguished, and we all settled down for what proved to be a very brief respite.

Before dawn, Dad awoke with one of the strange premonitions that rivermen are prone to. Struggling into his trousers, he hobbled out on deck to feel the air. A sinister streak of lightning slithered silently across the black sky, and Dad hurried to the steamboat to wake the crew and double the lines. In passing Spar-pole's door, he called through the screen, "Come on aft, we gotta bury a deadman!"

In the ensuing commotion, Spar-pole wasn't missed, but after the boats were secured, everyone headed for the galley for breakfast. When Spar-pole didn't appear, Dad went to his room to investigate and found it empty. There was a note on the pillow.

"Capn Billy. I do wan to be an akter but no enuf to hep with a merder. Yers truly. Spar-pole."

UP THE
MONONGAHELA

Our season opened in April, and the first month was spent going up and down the Monongahela and the Allegheny. The spring thaws always turned the banks of the southern rivers into a sea of adhesive mud, but the shale-covered shores of the coal mining territory assured the customers a firm footing.

The Monongahela was lined with forges, foundries, and coal tipples, ugly, black structures rising out of the equally ugly black, barren-looking earth. Everything was covered with coal dust, and even the steel-colored sky seemed to be permeated with the fine black film. At night, when the mills turned that same sky into a sea of red and the banks were dotted with gaping, flame-filled holes, the river became a perfect setting for Dante's *Inferno*.

The mines were ethnic melting pots with Poles, Hungarians, and Slovaks working side by side with Italians, Croations, and Serbs. When the showboat was landing, the men on the early shift were on their way to work, their miners' lanterns sticking out of their foreheads. They looked like a long line of ants, making their way along the mountainside to disappear into a hole in the ground.

At noon, a shrill whistle blew and children who sorted slag in the mines would rush to the river, screaming at each other in a mixture of strange tongues. Black with coal dust, the boys would pull off their heavy work shoes and wade out into the cold water.

The girls, who wore dark woolen dresses with long, black stockings, stood or sat shyly in little coveys on the riverbank, chewing on pieces of hard sausage or cheese. At the end of half an hour, the whistle blew again, and the children would scramble up the hill, over the top and out of sight.

The miners were friendly, generous people who loved the showboats. They came early and stayed late, sometimes bringing us food, a pot of this, a dish of that, colorful and pungent. Usually, the youngest in the family would make the presentation, curtsying with a shy smile. Then everyone would laugh, slap one another's shoulders, and shake our hands vigorously. The food was always delicious and what my father called "mysterious," but when it came to asking for recipes, we couldn't understand a word they said.

Invariably, the first person to come on board during the day would ask if we took scrip, a form of money issued by the owner of the mine. Though paper scrip has been used by the military for many years during wartime, circumstances surrounding the coal mining industry led to its being one of the largest private users of metal token money.

The coal camps were mostly in isolated mountainous areas with a spur railroad line and sometimes the river as their only means of transportation. There was no bank for many torturous miles, and the use of U.S. currency was not practical. Also scrip offered a bit of protection against the ever-present danger of robberies.

The miners lived in small, unpainted shacks that clung to the mountainside in a little cluster called the Patch. They paid their rent at the company store, where they also purchased food, clothing, and other necessities.

When a miner went to work at a mine, during the first week, he would ask for an advance on his salary. He would be given scrip, which was legal tender as long as it was spent on company goods or services. The amount advanced would be charged against the employee's payroll account. There was no place for the miners to live except in company-owned houses and no place to shop except in the company store.

In principle, the use of scrip was a convenient and viable answer to a unique problem, but it didn't take long for some of the mine owners to realize what potential profits lay in their monopolies. So the rents were set at the maximum, and the store carried the very best brands of merchandise with extremely high markups.

It was not unheard of for a company to make more from rental fees and store profits than it did in the operation of the coal mine. Nor was it unusual, at the end of a pay period, for a miner's deductions to exceed his amount of earnings. Sometimes a man would work for months without ever seeing a bit of hard cash.

In 1947, Merle Travis would write and sing a song that would be performed through the years by great stars like Tennessee Ernie Ford and Tom Jones. Its wailing, mournful melody complemented the words.

> You load sixteen tons, and what do you get?
> Another day older, and deeper in debt.
> St. Peter, don't you call me 'cause I can't go.
> I owe my soul to the company store.

The tokens were called different names—*flickers*, *light-weight*, and *doo lolly* (which is intriguing since *lolly* is a British slang term for money). They were usually made of brass in various shapes and sizes. Square, round, oval, some scalloped pieces, and some with cut-outs in the middle. Stamped with the company trademark and initials, some of them also carried the number of the mine. They were all marked to denote their value, from one cent to a dollar, but regardless of their purchasing power at the company store, a mile from the mine camp, in any direction, they were worthless. So the miner's visit to the showboat hung on the captain's answer to that question, "Do you take scrip?"

Dad always solved the problem by making arrangements with

Scrip, often used by coal-mining families (*left*); a pass, or "comp" (*top right*); a reserved seat ticket (*bottom right*)

the owner of the mine to have the company store opened after the show. That way, Dad could take a deckhand and an actor or two with him and spend all the scrip on supplies. Other times he would buy coal for the steamboat.

It would have been a pity for the miners to miss a show. They were fantastic audiences. It always amazed me to see how well they responded to the plays even though many of them spoke very little English. Occasionally, a wave of low murmurs would roll over the crowd as friends or family members translated, in half a dozen languages, what the actors were saying. They never lost interest and instinctively responded to the various moods of the play, crying, smiling, and laughing at all the appropriate times. Between the acts, when we sold prize candy, they bought it by the trayful and when the villain sang, the leading lady danced, or the character man did magic, they were delirious with joy.

January,
the bucking mule

One summer, Dad bought a trained bucking mule named January from a circus. January was a big gray beast with a short bristly mane and a disposition to match. His tail looked like a rope that was coming unraveled, and, according to his mood, his remarkably long ears stood up like a rabbit's, drooped like a bloodhound's, or laid back flat against his skeletal head.

Dad offered a five-dollar prize for anyone who would come up on stage and ride him for thirty seconds. We always held the contest at the end of the show, and Mother, at the piano, would pound out some lively music while the actors struck the set. Props and set pieces were hurriedly taken off to the greenroom, the backdrop was folded, and the wings were leaned against the bare back wall.

First, our deckhand would demonstrate how gentle the animal was. After unobtrusively giving January's left ear a twist as a cue to behave, he would mount and ride him around the stage, docile as a lamb. Then, members of the audience would be invited to do the same. Young men, anxious to show off for their ladies, would rush up through the box seats and wait in line. When their turn came, they would leap onto January's back, only to be tossed high and wide. Sometimes, a particularly lightweight boy would sail clear across the orchestra pit into the first row of seats.

No one ever finished the ride, until we took him up the Monongahela River. Dad had forgotten that mules were used in the mines. The first night seven contenders held on for the full time. It cost Dad thirty-five dollars in prize money. January did his best and he knew a lot of tricks. He bucked and kicked, twisted and turned, sat down, shook his head, bared his teeth and hee-hawed all the way through. He rolled his eyes, spun in circles, tried to bite their legs, and got down on his front knees. But those boys stuck on his back like cockleburs. After that we never held the contest in the coalfields. Those miners sure knew their mules.

As we came off the Monongahela onto the Ohio and headed downstream we moved between walls of apple-green willows, broken occasionally by stretches of pebbled beach. By now, the play was running smoothly, the actors were settled in their staterooms, and life had taken on the lovely, lazy pattern that could be found only on board a showboat in the spring.

For me, the day began before dawn as I woke to the sounds of shouted orders, running feet, and the creaks and groans of the stage plank, a gangplank that was rolled out to shore at each landing, being hauled aboard. I leaped out of bed, gave my face a token splash of cold water and struggled into my clothes. Then I walked quickly around the guard that ran the full length of the outside of the boat.

The cook always had a doughnut or a hot buttered biscuit ready for me and a little enamel bucket with a lid filled with coffee for my Dad, already in the pilot house. Clasping the handle of the bucket in one hand and wolfing the pastry as I ran, I retraced my steps to the showboat, hurried up the back stairs to the second deck, and gingerly climbed the ladder to the roof.

The pilot house sat close to the front of the boat, and the 120-foot walk over the tar paper roof was always a bit frightening. I never got close to the edge but stayed right in the middle with my eyes glued to Dad's back where he stood at the wheel.

Seemingly in response to my gaze, Dad would turn and wave, and as I climbed the four steps leading into the pilot house he would tie down the rudder by slipping a loop of rope, which was anchored to the floor, over one of the spokes of the pilot wheel. Then he would lift me up and set me on the high pilot stool. Putting his captain's hat on my head, he would take the coffee bucket. Then he would free the rudder and turn the wheel over to me with instructions to "keep 'er nose right on that point."

He would turn away with a false air of confidence, to pour his coffee into a mug while I kept a death grip on the wheel and trembled with delight. Then he would turn back to me and say, "She's driftin', honey. Pull 'er down right." He'd walk to the other side of the wheel and with one hand, help me move the giant four-cornered swan.

On the right front corner of the roof, with a flag at its tip, a long pole called a jack-staff stood tall and slender. It was used as a guide in steering. By spotting a landmark on shore, and lining up the jack-staff with it, you could plainly see when you were moving to the right or left. My spine always tingled when I saw the mammoth boat respond to the wheel.

Our trips usually took from two to three hours, but the time spent in that pilot house was never long enough for me. It was my very own magic carpet, my castle, my playhouse, my school. It was there that I first came to grips with arithmetic, learning to count the buoys that floated in the river to mark the outline of the channel and the government beacon lights along the bank. Every now and then Dad would slip me a dose of history, sweetened with a teaspoon of legend. "Look there," he'd say. "That's where Chief Blackbird is buried, sittin' straight up on the back of his horse!" or "We're comin' into Ripley, Ohio. That was one of the most important stations of the Underground Railway during the Civil War. Right down there is where the real Eliza escaped over the ice."

Of course, my favorite subject was the river itself. Dad knew every creek, crossing, slough, and sandbar from the head of the Alleghany to the upper Mississippi. He could even read the ripples in the water and tell by its color and waves its depth and rate of speed. Just above Dog Island, at the mouth of the Cumberland River, he'd say, "Now watch, honey. You put your jack-staff on that big sycamore tree and keep your stern on that little red schoolhouse, and it'll take you right through this Old Maid's Crossing." My head swam with names of sandbars and gravel bars like Petticoat Ripple, Sunfish Bar, and Owl Hollow Run.

Twice each year we passed Bryant's Landing, just below Manchester Island, and though I knew it wasn't named in my personal honor, just having Dad point it out was enough to set my dreamer's mind afloat and make me beg for stories about the Four Bryants and how they came to the rivers.

PERENNIAL PALS

It had been over twenty-five years since the Four Bryants had made their first tour of the Ohio River on *Price's New Water Queen*, but the river was basically the same. Willow-lined shores, sleepy little towns with friendly people, steamboats puffing past, and here and there a shantyboat tied to a cottonwood tree.

At almost every town we played, some boy always seemed to be waiting on the top of the bank, and as we came into sight, he would throw his hat in the air and run along the horizon shouting, "HERE COMES THE SHOWBOAT!!!!!"

Dad would take the wheel, slip a looped rope over one of the spokes to hold it steady, and grab the bell pull to signal the engineer. If the landing had not yet recovered from the spring thaw, it would be a sea of mud and would have to be approached with caution.

Dad would leave the pilot house and hurry to the edge of the tar paper roof. Leaning his body out over the edge and holding a cardboard megaphone to his mouth he would shout, "Dad! Get the springline! Charlie! On the stern! Ready with that headline! JUMP, LEO, JUMP!"

On that cry, Leo would leap out into the air from the deck below. Dressed in a pair of ancient blue jeans with one end of a two-and-a-half-inch hawser tied around his waist, he would land feet first in the shallow water and nearly disappear from sight.

Putting out the stage plank

Billy (*right*) and a deckhand at a landing

Struggling like a netted gar, he would manage to get his footing on the treacherous bottom, but he was twenty feet from the bank and chest-deep in river mud. Laboriously, he would make his way through the adhesive ooze. Upon reaching the willow-lined shore, he would grab an overhanging branch to pull himself to solid ground and lay quietly for a moment breathing deeply.

"Tie her off to that cottonwood!" Dad would shout. "Shorty! Get that spar-pole out!" Leo would pull himself to his feet and begin wrapping the big rope around the bole of the tree.

By this time, the little boy on shore would be back and with him a group of children, friends I saw for only one day out of each year. Lined along the top of the riverbank, they would dance and wave and clap their hands. At least one of the boys would be astride a fat Shetland pony and another would climb to the very top of a swaying cottonwood, wave his hat in the air, and yell, redundantly, "HERE COMES THE SHOWBOAT!!!!!"

Dad would be leaving the roof now. I would follow him down the ladder and race ahead of him, around the guard to the front deck. Then I would stand, hopping from one foot to the other while they put out the stage plank, drove a long iron bar into the mud at its end to keep it from shifting, and then laid planks over the mud from there to the solid shore.

As soon as Dad nodded approval, I would race to shore and up the bank to the troupe of waiting children, my perennial playmates who looked forward to our annual visit almost as much as I did. We would spend most of the morning wading along the shore, playing duck-on-the-rock, chasing pollywogs in inland pools, skipping rocks, or fishing for shiners with bent-pin hooks. Before noon, Dad would come off the boat to walk to the village for mail and groceries. I would go along with my entire entourage. Usually, the equestrian would gallantly walk and lead his pony, with me riding in style.

Along the way, we would hand out show bills for the night's performance. When we returned to the boats the big bell usually rang for dinner, so we went on board. My faithful followers would scatter to their homes, calling out promises for a quick return. By the time I had finished eating the midday meal they would all be back. I introduced them to Leo, by then bathed and dressed in clean clothes.

Leo was half Cherokee Indian. He joined the showboat two months before I did, and he would remain with it until the day it would be sold. At different times he worked as a deckhand, fireman, watchman, bill-poster, and actor. He was also my bodyguard and my friend.

In the afternoons, when I played with the children, Leo would always be a few yards behind us, walking silently like a protective spirit. He never entered into our games or interfered with our plans, just stood nearby with his arms folded across his chest, watching us with eyes like anthracite.

Sometimes he would heel-sit, leaning back against a big rock or the trunk of a tree, but he was always there if I needed him, and many's the time he fished me out of the river with a pike-pole when I built one of my falls-apart-as-soon-as-it-hits-the-water rafts.

His was no easy task, for my young companions were fearless and my toys were bigger than life. The deserted dance floors of idle excursion boats were our skating rinks, and wharf houses, filled with empty egg crates waiting to be shipped up or down river, were our play houses. With those crates we built miles of tunnels that crossed and recrossed in an exciting labyrinth permeated with the musty odor of straw and chickens. Of course, there was always the river to float on, swim in, or fish from.

The river itself never frightened me. I could jump into unknown depths of water and swim as far out as I was allowed. Only one aspect of it held a strange mixture of fascination and terror for me—the "step-off."

Step-offs were deep holes in the bottom of the river which seemed to have been scooped out. You could be walking in waist-deep water on solid ground, often quite close to shore, when, without warning, one step would plunge you into what felt like a bottomless pit. Off balance, you would sink like a rock, and the water would be dark and cold. There was no unusual pull or undercurrent and you would eventually resurface, but the sensation of suddenly being thrust into a wet void was horrendous.

Even if I walked out from the shore into the water and someone on the boat or on the bank called out, "Be careful, Betty, there's a step-off out there," my knees would weaken and my heart would go into a buck dance. I never completely lost my fear of them, but some advice from Dad did help. "All you have to do when you fall into a step-off, is just tread water, and keep calm. The current will carry you along until you get your bearings. Then you can swim to shore." He smiled and added, "Life's full of step-offs, honey, both in the water and on dry land. Just remember the rules: float and *don't panic!*"

On rainy days we played inside the showboat—hide-and-seek between the rows of seats or follow-the-leader under the stage and into the damp hull where we held our ears to gunnels, listening to the water that rushed below. Now and then a congenial performer would treat us to a private performance of juggling, wire-walking, or magic.

At five o'clock the supper bell would ring and the children would hurry home to get ready to be in the audience for the night's performance. After supper I would get cleaned up and put on my makeup as the actors set the stage for the show. We used grease paint for a base. Lipstick was called "lip rouge." It came in a tiny round tin box and was put on with a pinkie. It was also used for blush. A slight dab of it on each cheek bone would be spread and blended with upward and outward strokes.

The eyes were a work of art. Eye shadow in various colors came in little logs wrapped in wax paper and encased in heavy cardboard tubes. It too was applied with a finger. Eyeliner was drawn on under the eye and along the edge of the upper lid with a toothpick dipped into mascara. The two lines would meet at the outer corner of the eye and extend about a quarter of an inch upward. The effect was referred to as "doe eyes."

Mascara was a six-inch roll of black, waxlike makeup. We would break off a chunk of it and place it in a tiny tin skillet. This we held over a lit candle until the mascara melted. Then, we rolled the end of a kitchen match over and over in the melted mascara until a wad of it formed. With this, we painted our eye lashes, giving them first a base coat, letting it dry, and then, by the same process, adding a little bulb on the end of each individual eyelash. This was called "beading."

Mother would then attack my hair, which was as straight as a poker. She had two answers to the problem, rag curlers and a curling iron. At night, before I went to bed, she would separate my hair into small sections. Then she would dampen one clump, tie a strip of rag at its roots, wind the hair around the rag, and tie both ends of the rag together. She would repeat the process on one section at a time until my entire head was covered with knotted rags. The next morning she would untie and remove them and violà! Shirley Temple!

The curls took a bit of a beating during the day, so after I had my makeup on, Mother would rejuvenate them by brushing and brushing each one around her forefinger till they all gleamed. The curling iron, another instrument of torture during the twenties, would take care of any errant bits of hair that she missed. The iron looked like a pair of scissors with round, iron blades. They had no heating element, so Mother would light the coal oil lamp, bend out one side of a large hair pin and hook the straight side over the edge of the chimney. Then she would clamp the blades of the iron to the bent part of the hair pin.

After a short wait, she would lift out the iron, lick her finger, and dab at the hot end. If it spit and sizzled it was ready. She would then proceed to clasp any loose bits of hair in it and wind it tightly.

When the hair began to smell scorched, *I* was ready. It probably took Lon Chaney less time to prepare for a performance.

At seven-thirty the dynamo, or generator, on the steamboat roared to life and hundreds of bulbs lit up, outlining the showboat in the night like a floating fairyland. People began coming down the straw path, their lanterns bobbing and weaving like a queue of fireflies. It seemed as though they were all laughing as they boarded the boat. My little friends were scrubbed to tender point, and they grinned and giggled self-consciously in their dress clothes. They bought their tickets through the office window. Every now and then someone would hold up for our approval a baby born since our last visit.

When the final customers had been ushered to their seats, the office was closed and Mother and I made a mad dash for the orchestra pit to play the overture. She played piano, and I played drums or saxophone. Mother's favorite arrangement was "Maple Leaf Rag."

A flash of the footlights told us that the play was ready to begin, and Mother glided into soft mood music while the roll curtain slowly ascended. Then we ducked under the stage to emerge in the greenroom and await our cue.

My friends came to see me perform, but it wasn't unusual for them to have me sell them a ticket, usher them to their seats, play drums for them in the overture, portray a sickly child on stage, dance for them after the first act, die for them in the second act, came back to life to sell them a box of candy, and go to heaven for them in the third act.

At the end of the show Mother rushed back to the piano to "play the people out." I would be on the front deck, selling souvenir postcards and saying farewell to that group of my perennial playmates. I could hear my mother pounding out "Smile, Darn You Smile!" and the crowd responded to her musical command.

People always lingered, reluctant to leave. They would talk with the family and shake our hands. But finally, the last members of the audience would cross the gangplank, light their lanterns, and slowly make their way homeward through the night.

Makeup would be removed and the wardrobe hung away, the dynamo would come to a grumbling halt, and darkness would settle on my world. I'd lie in bed listening to the night sounds of the river. Crickets chirruped, bullfrogs buck-upped, and trout splashed in the channel.

I thought of the people who had shared their lives with us that day. Somehow I felt sad to realize that they were gone for another year. And yet, I knew we would remain in their thoughts, for the showboat was an integral part of their lives, bringing them the opportunity to make believe and buy a once-a-year ticket to "Never Never Land."

SCREECHING
PIPE OF PAN

In the early years, before I was born, the only form of advertisement showboats had was handbills the captain would mail ahead to the postmaster, along with a few passes to the show. The postmaster would tack up one bill among the "Wanted" posters and take another to the feed store. The rest he would give to his mail carrier to deliver along the rural route.

As more and more showboats came along, with no idea of each other's schedule or whereabouts, it wasn't unusual for two boats, one headed up stream and one down, to "day and date." They would nose in together at the same wharf, send their bands to parade side by side up and down the main street, and send their calliope players up top to try to drown each other out.

As more boats were built and competition increased, the billposter, or advance man, came into his own. This man was sent out at the beginning of the season with a few dollars in his pocket, a book of passes, and all the paper (posters, tack cards, and "three sheets") he could carry. After being told to "pick up more paper at Fraziers Bottom," he became the forgotten man, expected to live by his wits.

On land, he traveled by mule, horse and buggy, bicycle, or shanks mare (walking). On the water, by raft, skiff, or motorboat.

He would go into town, present a landlady with two complimentary tickets referred to as "comps" and receive in return a night's lodging, breakfast, and a bucket of paste made from flour and water. With that, he would post bills on barns, trees, fences, or any available surface.

Between towns, he could usually find a dry barn or haystack to sleep in. Often, farmers invited him to a meal, and when they didn't he might "find" an egg or even a chicken that he could cook over an open fire. Should he become really destitute, the paste could be made into an edible if tasteless breakfast which became know as "bill-poster pancakes."

Some of the show bills were printed to advertise a specific show like *Uncle Tom's Cabin* or *Ten Nights in a Barroom*, but some of them were more generic in design. Thus, a picture of a man in Western attire, leading a horse, or talking with a young lady wearing a long loose dress called a Mother Hubbard and a sun bonnet, could be used for *Trail of the Lonesome Pine*, *The Cowboy*, *Girl of the Golden West*, or any of a half a dozen other plays.

But no matter how pertinent to the actual offering some showboat paper was, it always carried testimonials to the show's wholesomeness. The bills were liberally salted with words like *cultivated*, *clean*, *moral*, and *refined*. They were also colorful, dramatic, and romantic. They set the imagination soaring, and while waiting for the actual arrival of the showboat, people looked at them again and again, reveling in their promises of future delights.

However, though the posting of paper in advance was of great importance to the showboat, no printed matter of any color or form could electrify people like the magical voice of a steam calliope. Show bills announced that the showboat would arrive at some future date. The calliope screamed immediacy! "HERE COMES THE SHOWBOAT!" it shrieked. "RIGHT NOW!"

The calliope was invented by a farmer by the name of Joshua Stoddard of Worchester, Massachusetts. It made its first public appearance, appropriately, on the Fourth of July, 1855. It was very successful, but its caterwauling must have given rise to questions about its name: calliope, (ka-li-o-pe), from the Greek word meaning sweet-voiced or magnificent-voiced. And the muse of epic poetry must cringe at hearing her name pronounced cal-ee-ope by river and circus people alike.

Stoddard immediately organized the American Steam Company but lost the business within five years to Arthur S. Denny, who later claimed to have invented the calliope himself. After being bandied about by men with various ideas of how the instrument could be useful, it was picked up by the circuses and then the river boats, where it found its true home. Its ear-splitting, mezmerizing melodies were perfect as an advertising medium for the bawdy, boisterous trade of the packets.

Within a year, every steamer that could boast Texas space had one, and, in 1858, when the Union Line of Packets advertised "an instrument on every boat," an Iowa paper announced, "The Missouri River is now the most musical stream of the world."

After the Civil War, the showboats adopted the calliope as their own and used it not only as a screeching pipe of Pan but to furnish distilled drinking water, which was kept in a wooden water cooler just outside the galley door. Calliope water was soft and flat, a little like well water. Some people on our boat had difficulty getting used to the taste, and they would pour it back and forth from one bucket to another, claiming that it lacked air.

Our calliope was one of the loudest on the rivers. It took a hundred and twenty pounds of steam pressure to bring it to life, and it could be heard for ten miles. Its clarion call floated across the fields, through the valleys, and up the hills. It carried with it the power to empty schools, close stores, and lure farmers from the fields. Women left bread baking in the oven and old people struggled from their rockers and hobbled and hopped to the levee, waving their canes and shouting with glee. It captured imaginations, stirred hearts, and lived for years in the memory of anyone fortunate enough to fall under the spell of its unique sound.

One legend tells of a woman in jail on the Bayou Teche in Louisiana—the only woman ever to be hanged in that state—whose

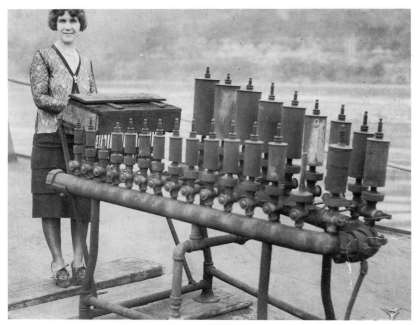

Josephine at the calliope

last request was to hear a calliope play "Nearer My God To Thee."
They say that the governor commuted her sentence to fall when the
first showboat arrived that far south.

Another well-known tale is that on every boat that passed the
penitentiary on the upper Mississippi, the captain had the calliope
player play "The Prisoner's Song" for its composer, who was behind
those bleak walls. For years, engineers at their posts, pilots at the
wheels, or deckhands stretched out on the guards would invariably
sing softly as they glided past the prison.

> If I had the wings of an angel,
> Over these prison walls I would fly.
> I'd fly to the arms of my loved one
> And there I'd be willing to die.

For all their mystical qualities, calliopes were difficult to play.
The keys were hard to push down. Occasionally a wire would break

or a valve jam. They were usually played by men. Mother was one of the few women to conquer the instrument. A page from her journal of 1915 describes her first meeting with the monstrosity. She had just joined the showboat as a piano player and was surprised to find she was expected to play the calliope as well. Of that day, she wrote:

> This afternoon, I got my first look at the strangest musical instrument I have ever seen. It has twenty-four whistles mounted upright on a V-shaped pipe and sits on four iron legs. There is a key board at the wide end of the V and each whistle is attached to one of the metal keys by strong but flexible wires.
>
> It is played like a piano but the keyboard has only twenty-four keys. The lowest note is C and the highest note is E. The E-flat and A-flat are missing. The keys were all loose and wiggled over the keyboard. Then, when the engineer turned on the steam, there was a loud screech and every key popped up to a level.
>
> I tried pressing one of them down and couldn't even budge it. Then, I struck a full chord and it relieved the pressure. The Calliope is terribly out of tune and the chord sounded like a quartet of factory whistles.
>
> Steam flew and the coal soot blew. I struck another chord and then started to play "In the Good Old Summer Time." My hat blew off my head, my hair blew into my eyes and I thought my ear drums would split. But I played a whole chorus of the song and I've kept the job!

There has never been a more Sirenlike sound than that of the lilting strains of calliope music floating across the miles. But standing toe to toe with a calliope at full power is another thing entirely. Still, I never missed one of Mother's concerts if I was within running distance of the roof when she started to play.

She wore asbestos gloves because the brass keys got very hot. Rubber boots, a floor-length black slicker, and a sou'wester protected her from the steam which condensed in the air and fell upon her like hot rain. She would lean down and open the main valve, causing the steam to hiss and the whistles to whimper as the pipes came to life. Then, walking around to the keyboard, she would take two wads of cotton from the pocket of her slicker and stuff them into her ears. Mother would pull the hat low over her eyes, grimace, and press down on the metal keys. The first shrill chord always sent shivers up my spine and a sharp pain into my jaw behind the ears.

She always began by playing "Here Comes the Showboat." I would cover my ears and jump up and down at the exquisite sound. Then she played "There'll Be a Hot Time in the Old Town Tonight," "Dark Town Strutters Ball," "Oh, Johnny," and "Steamboat Bill."

Every now and then she would disappear in a dense cloud of white steam, and, unable to control myself, I would start turning forbidden cartwheels right there on the roof. Suddenly, she would slip into a waltz.

> Let me call you sweetheart.
> I'm in love . . . with . . . you . . .

She always closed her fifteen-minute concert with a reprieve of

> Here comes the showboat! Here comes the showboat!
> Huff puff puff puff puff puff puffin' along!

Then, suddenly, it was over, ending as abruptly as it had begun and, for a moment, the silence was almost painful. My heart seemed to be encased in a bubble of air, and I could feel the ghosts of the melodies floating around my head. The black iron monster whistled a protest and the soaring steam settled reluctantly as mother shut off the valves.

The greatest mental picture of a calliope in action that I have ever experienced was conjured up by a story that Dad used to tell on the showboat. "Many years ago," he would begin, "a showboat went way, way up the Kentucky River carrying the first calliope to be seen or heard in that territory.

"A mountain man, with his six-year-old son was out hunting. They were walking the ridge of the high riverbank when the showboat rounded the bend and hove into sight. The calliope player was up top, and the calliope was puffin' steam and screaming like a banshee.

"As the showboat came even with the man and boy, the mountaineer raised his gun to his shoulder and blasted away at the fearful varmint.

"The calliope player couldn't hear the shot but he saw the gun and the puff of smoke, and when the man aimed again, the player ran to the edge of the roof and jumped overboard. The calliope was still puffing steam and screeching through a stuck valve when the player hit the water.

"The little boy looked up and asked, 'Did you kill it, Paw?' The man shook his head and said, "'Nope, but I sure made it let go of that man!'"

DOWN BY THE
O-HI-O

We started our annual tour on the Ohio by playing the Pennsylvania towns of Sewickley, Freedom, Shippingport, and Empire. Then on to New Cumberland, West Virginia; Toronto, Ohio; Mingo Junction, Ohio; Short Creek, West Virginia; Tiltonville, Martins Ferry, Pipe Creek, Powhatan Point, and Clarington, Ohio.

Mother made a note in her journal one season at Clarington. "Thought Betty had the measles but it was heat rash from playing on the sand pile."

At that time, there was a large industry in dredging sand and gravel from the riverbed. After screening and washing it, the dredgers would sell it to contractors for making concrete. While waiting to be shipped in sand barges to the buyers, the dredgings would be kept in huge piles, high on the bank. They were wonderful pyramids of sand which I climbed up, slid down, and burrowed into.

After leaving Clarington, we went to Proctor and Sistersville, West Virginia. Then on to New Matamoras and Murphys Landing, Ohio; St. Mary's and Belmont, West Virginia; and Reno, Ohio. In one of those towns, in 1927, we went to visit a hatchery. The owner had invited us to see the baby chickens and ducks. The eggs were on trays which could be pulled out of the incubator to check the hatching progress. As we were standing there looking at them, the owner drew out one tray and an egg rolled over the edge to the floor. It broke and disgorged a baby duck. The owner picked it up and gave it to me with instructions on how to care for it. We took it back to the boat and, within a few days, the duckling was not only walking around but following me closer than my shadow.

From then on, when we went for the mail or groceries, "Dandy" went along. If the town was big enough for sidewalks, the duckling would follow me to the crossing and plop down off the curb. But once across the street, he found he couldn't jump up, so he would run around the corner, chasing us in the gutter, on the tips of his webbed toes, "peeping" at the top of his lungs. When he came to a ramp he would scurry up it, get behind me, and continue our stroll in silence.

We played Marietta, Ohio, at the mouth of the Muskingum River. Then came Parkersburg, West Virginia, followed by the Ohio towns of Belpre, Hockingport, Reedsville, and Long Bottom. For the next few days we skipped back and forth across the river from Ravenswood, West Virginia, to Racine, Ohio; New Haven, West Virginia; and Pomeroy, Ohio. Then we held to the Ohio side for Middleport, Cheshire, and Addison, swinging back to West Virginia to play Point Pleasant, the town that had been and still is such an important place in the Bryant family's lives.

Here we would turn up the Kanawha River to Leon and Buffalo, West Virginia. At Buffalo, I remember a little girl named June. Her father, Mr. J.O. Donohoe and his brother Memphis, owned and operated the Buffalo Department Store where Dad always bought supplies. It had carbide lights that looked like electricity, and, for a while, it also housed the post office. When the town built a new post office Charles Raynes put his funeral parlor on that side of the store.

After Buffalo, we went up to Poca, St. Albans, Dunbar, and South Charleston. In those days, we felt Charleston proper was too big a city for us. We played Dana, Marmet, Winefrede, Dickenson, Coalburg, and Cedar Grove. Then, Crown Hill, Pratt, and Handley.

There we would turn around and repeat the same route back to the Ohio River, playing a different show.

We always stopped at the beautiful little town of Gallipolis, Ohio, boyhood home of the famous writer Oscar Odd McIntyre, known to his readers as O.O. McIntyre. From 1912 to 1940, he wrote a syndicated column called "New York Day by Day," which was carried in hundreds of newspapers around the world. He was a very close friend of Dad's and a great supporter of our showboat.

Going on down the Ohio, we played Bladen, Ohio; Ashton, West Virginia; Athalia, Ohio; Proctorville, Ohio; Huntington, West Virginia; Catlettsburgh, West Virginia; Sheridan Ohio; and Ironton, Ohio, where I was christened at St. Joseph's Catholic Church in 1922. In 1939, I received my high school diploma from their school. Between those two dates, I met Richard Schreiber, who was to become a distinguished man of letters and to remain a lifelong friend.

We played Greenup, Kentucky, and I remember a young boy there who had a pony named Gypsy. After Greenup was Lloyd, Kentucky; Fullerton, Kentucky; and Portsmouth, Ohio. At that point, between Ravenswood and Portsmouth, we had passed seven movable dams in two weeks.

In 1929, President Herbert Hoover spoke at the dedication of the Ohio River Nine Foot Canalization Project, during which nearly fifty movable dams had been built between Emsworth, Pennsylvania, to a point ten miles below Joppa, Illinois. The object was to maintain a constant navigable depth of at least nine feet throughout the entire length of the Ohio River. President Hoover compared it in scope and cost to the construction of the Panama Canal.

I never tired of watching the process of "locking through," and I never lost the feeling of awe that came over me each time we headed for a lock chamber. No matter where I was when Dad blew for passage, I hurried to the pilot house on the top deck.

Dad would pull the whistle cord twice, two low, mournful blasts. From the lock wall another whistle would answer, a single

Locking through

high shriek that said, "Come ahead!" Lining up our jack-staff with the lock's flag pole, Dad would ease the boats in. The big gates would shut behind us. If we were going downstream, the water would be let out slowly, and on a watery elevator we would slowly descend into the dark shadows of the cavern. The dripping, cement walls seemed to rise around us. I would shudder as we neared the bottom and were engulfed by the cold, damp air. Finally we would come to a stop, the gates ahead would grind open, and we would glide out into the sunshine, like in the happy ending of a fairy tale.

If we were traveling upstream, the process was reversed. Dad would pilot the boats into the chamber, the gates would close, and the cascading waters would raise us slowly to the very rim of the deep cement canyon.

The lockmaster, with his family, lived in a house on the top of the manmade mounds. And he always had a motley collection of long-eared dogs. Every time a boat would blow for a lock, the dogs would set up a howl. With flapping ears, wagging tails, and wet, dangling tongues, they would hurry down the long line of stone steps to bark greetings to the deckhands and beg food scraps from the cook.

Each steamboat had a whistle with a tone that was distinctly its own, and man or woman, child or dog could tell from many miles away which boat was approaching. One packet boat had a notorious reputation for poor pay and, consequently, poor cooks. As the story went, the food on board was so bad that the lockmaster's dogs refused to come out when she blew for a lockage.

After Portsmouth, there was Buena Vista, Ohio; Vanceburg, Kentucky; Stout, Ohio; Wrightsville, Ohio. And then came Manchester, Ohio, site of a button factory. Each time we pulled in there to land, if I was in the pilot house with Dad he would say, "All right, now, button, button, who's got the button?" I would pretend to think hard and then shout, "MANCHESTER!" We both laughed as though we really had said something funny.

During the Great Depression hundreds of men, women, and children found their way to the rivers. Once there, they would build tiny houseboats and equip them with ropes, lanterns, fishing gear, and garden tools. Then, pushing the little craft out into the channel, each family would float leisurely down the river, a happy part of that group of aquatic nomads who were known as shantyboaters.

If they came to a town where someone was hiring, they would nose into shore and tie up among the willows. The men would work in the mill, potteries, or orchards, and the women would cultivate tiny gardens at the water's edge. When the work ran out, they would load the pike pole and fish nets on top of their little boat and store the produce and the garden tools in the hull. Then, after tying up the dogs on the front porch of the boat and calling to the children to get aboard, they would cast off and drift silently downstream to the next landing of opportunity.

When there was no work to be had on shore, they could always stop at a sandbar and fish or they could drag for mussels. We could always tell when we were getting close to Manchester, because the riverbanks were lined with little ricky-ticky boats which were the homes of shellers who dragged for freshwater mussels for a living.

Though most of the button industry was located up the Illinois, around Muscatine, Manchester, Ohio, also attracted workers to its button factory. Dozens of tiny, weather-beaten crafts of every description would be strung out along the shore. Moored end to end, they were tied so closely to each other that it was possible to stroll for a mile stepping from deck to deck all the way.

Some of the cabins were made from packing-case material, with weird-looking, crooked stovepipes sticking out of their roofs and sides at all angles. Most of them had their names written in twisted, green willow branches, dried and mounted on the prow. Names like *My Home*, *Petes Palace*, *Oh you Kid*, and *Rolypoly*.

I loved watching the musselers work. The women would set up a heavy, wooden table flanked on either side by a tin tub and a wooden bin. They would build a fire early in the morning and make coffee and bacon sandwiches for their families. Then, the women would hang a big black kettle filled with river water over the fire. The men and boys would climb into their flat-bottomed johnboats and pole out to the shoals.

The mussels, freshwater mollusks much like clams, lay with half-open valves, in beds of sand or gravel under shallow water. Sometimes during the night, the river would take a sudden drop of as much as forty feet. Hundreds of mussels would be stranded on a vast expanse of smooth, shiny mud. They would roll on their edges, extend their muscles instinctively toward the water, and then pull the shells over their bodies. Laboriously, the mussels would inch their way across the mud toward the river, leaving behind a straight, thin-lined trail. Within minutes the muddy plain would be etched like a giant map of the universe.

The johnboats floated with the current, dragging alongside a brail or grab. The grab was a six-foot piece of iron pipe with a rope at each end for the musseler to hang on to. Along the pipe, pieces of trotline about three feet long hung down at six-inch intervals. Dull wire, twisted into tri-pronged hooks called crow foots, was tied to the lines. The pipe dragged these crude hooks over the mussels, which clamped their valves shut as soon as they were touched. When the brail was hauled up, the mussels, sometimes as many as a half a bushel, were dislodged and tossed into the bottom of the boat.

When the boat was full, the mussels were taken to shore and put in the boiling water. After a few seconds, they were drained and laid out on the table. The women split open the shells and tore out the meat. They tossed the shells into the bin and examined the mussels for pearls.

The pearls they produced ranged from small, imperfect slugs to one that occasionally brought as much as a hundred dollars to the finder. The meat was sold to farmers for pig and chicken feed, the shells to button factories known as saw-works. After the buttons had been cut, the perforated shells were broken into pieces to be used like gravel on the roads.

In the factories, the button cutters gave names to nearly forty different varieties of mussels. Arkansas, blue-point, buckhorn, bull-head, butterfly, creeper, deer-toe, dromedary, egg-shell, elephant ear, floater, hatchet-back, heel-splitter, hickory-nut, higgins-eye, kidney-shell, ladyfinger, maple leaf, monkey face, mucket, mud-shell, pancake, paper-shell, pit toe, pimple-back, pistol grip, pocketbook, rabbit foot, rock-shell, sand-shell, sheep-nose, spectacle-case, spike, squawfoot, stranger, three ridge, warty-back, and washboard.

Although there seems to be very little information about shantyboaters for our historians to work with, they were a viable part of our cultural history, an interesting group of people with a unique lifestyle. In 1929 when the government completed the federal lock and dam system which gave the river a nine-foot pool stage, many of the mussel beds were destroyed.

New flood walls and superhighways took many miles of possible landing spots, and new laws requiring all boats to have licenses scattered the remaining shantyboaters like startled minnows. Eventually, the colorful, friendly shantyboaters, who for years competed with the pollywogs for the murky waters beneath mosquito-infested willows, faded into the twilight of legendry.

Following our Manchester stop was Aberdeen, Ohio, and then Maysville, Kentucky, and therein lies another tale. Sixteen tails to be exact.

It's common knowledge that actors have always felt a kinship with animals, and they usually carry some sort of pet with them at all times. Dogs, cats, canaries, budgies, and even monkeys have been trooped across country with actors who often excused their presence by claiming they were "part of the act."

It was no different on the showboat. The whole family liked animals, and Dad was especially fond of dogs. Over the years I had goldfish, birds, rabbits, baby chicks, ducks, a bantam rooster, a pony, a Scotch terrier, a fox Terrier, and a slew of other dogs of more dubious lineage.

One spring at Maysville, Dad went to the sheriff's office to pay for our license. He found three large dogs confined to a cage. He asked the sheriff why they were there and was told they were strays and that unless they could be placed in homes they would have to be shot. The sheriff was a kind man who didn't look forward to destroying the dogs, so he asked Dad if we could take them out of town and try to find homes for them downriver. Dad didn't hesitate a minute, and as soon as the dogs were outfitted with rope leashes he brought them back to the boat.

I was delighted, especially when Dad gave me the privilege of naming them. They were all three females and very well mannered. One was obviously part airedale with a long, square jaw and floppy ears. I named her Muffin, as in ragamuffin. Another had long, thick hair which, if de-burred and bathed, would have been a golden color. Her I named Moonbeam.

The last one was big and fat, multicolored and heavy-coated. One ear stood up and the other hung down. She kept wagging a long, feathery tail that had absolutely no sense of direction, and she moved slowly, sitting down at every opportunity. I couldn't think of a name for her, but mother had no trouble at all. She took one look and said, *"That* one you can call 'Useless.'"

The next day, when Dad went for groceries in the next town, he told the owner of the store about the dogs. That afternoon the owner's wife and son came down to the boat and picked out Moonbeam. It was love at first sight for the boy, and his mother assured me that the dog would be well cared for and would retain the name of Moonbeam.

On the second day, a man who came to the boat early to buy tickets was happy to take Muffin home with him. That left Useless.

Dad figured to find a home for her on the third day, but when he went to the engine room to get her, Useless had disappeared. The rope she had been tied up with was gnawed through. We searched for her all day but finally gave up, deciding she had run away to the hills.

When we pulled out the next morning I cried because we hadn't found Useless a home, but my tears were wasted. That afternoon, behind the balcony seats, I went into a closet where we kept costumes and props, and there on the floor, in a nest of satin and velvet, I found Useless and thirteen little squirming, squeaking puppies.

We kept the family together for six weeks. Then, Useless decided that she had had enough of motherhood and stopped nursing them. That night, after the curtain came down on the last act and before mother started the chaser music, Dad stepped out in front of the curtain with a pup in his hands. He explained what had happened and said we were offering the puppy to anyone who would give it a good home. Usually, more than one hand was raised. Dad would solve that problem by passing out little slips of paper to each volunteer with instructions for them to write their names. Then,

Dad would gather them up and put them in his straw hat. I would come on stage and draw out a slip of paper.

Invariably, the person who won would hold the pup high, announce its appropriate name, and carry it out of the auditorium to a rousing round of applause. At the end of two weeks all the pups had been given away, but we still had Useless. Finally, our deckhand solved the problem by going to Dad and explaining that his ma and pa had a farm just a little bit further down the river. He said they loved dogs and if we could get Useless to them he knew they would give her a good home.

The next day was Sunday, and, as we never did a show on Sunday, Dad told the deckhand we would pull in at his family's farm and spend the night. We got there just after sunrise and the young man took Useless and disappeared over the riverbank. He came back just after supper carrying a basket from his mother. It held four homemade blackberry pies. He said the dog was fine and his folks loved her, but he hoped I wouldn't mind that they had changed her name to Lady.

I didn't mind a bit, I didn't think a dog should be called Useless when she had not only gotten us the best dessert we'd had all season but had also fixed it so that somewhere along the Ohio River, thirteen towns had thirteen dogs and every one of them was named "Showboat."

Put Them All Together, They Spell "Huckster"

Ripley, Ohio; Higginsport, Ohio; Augusta, Kentucky; Boudes Ferry, Ohio; Utopia, Ohio; Chilo, Ohio; and Moscow, Ohio. We usually arrived in Moscow on a Sunday and stayed till Monday when we did the show. We always had dinner that Sunday at the home of a lady friend of mother's, who served heavenly chicken dinners to paying guests. In the back yard she had a huge rose arbor that seemed to go on forever.

Mother was an outgoing person with an effervescent personality and a legion of friends. If she went to someone's home for a visit and they had a piano in the house, she would play and sing at the drop of a request. She was a very busy woman but could always find time for her favorite hobby, talking. Dad often said, "If Josie couldn't find anyone else, she would start a conversation with a store dummy."

Mother played piano for the overture, cue, or mood music, the actors' specialties, community singing, and chaser music at the end of the show. She played calliope concerts three times a day, one on our arrival, again around two o'clock in the afternoon, and finally in the evening about an hour before show time.

Mother handled all the concessions. She popped corn, bagged it, and made lemonade. She ordered prize candy from the Casey Candy Company in Chicago, unpacked the "flash" prizes, set them up on the stage for display, and put the prize tickets in the candy boxes, one to every ten. She paid the actors their commissions for selling candy and saw that Lady Violet got her share of the profits.

Mother had never been on stage as an actress before she joined the showboat, but once there, she trod the boards as fearlessly as a born trouper. She played every type of role from a Sis Hopkins, in broad comedy, to the longsuffering Lady Isabel in *East Lynne*. But her favorite part was a heavy, or villainess. She saw, with immediate clarity, what Bette Davis and Joan Crawford would discover years later, that while the villainess never won out in the end, she did get to emote through three acts with the best lines, the strongest scenes, and the prettiest wardrobe.

Mother loved to dress in beautiful and dramatic clothes. Her favorites were floor-length, black velvets with more feathers and plumes than you would see at a Mae West look-alike contest. In such an outfit and with a line such as "You contemptible cur, if you ever again even so much as attempt to thwart my plans, I give you my solemn oath, you shall live to rue the day!" Mother would nearly take wing on her exit.

She repaired props and wardrobe, tidied the greenroom and swept the stage. She did beadwork, crocheted, embroidered, knitted, and sewed. She swam, hiked, rode horseback, bicycled, and danced. She read books, wrote letters, did typing for Dad, and took care of whatever pets I had currently in tow. She practiced her piano, learned her lines, occasionally sang, and made hats. She was totally tireless, had the energy of an eight-year-old boy, and talked like a Gatling gun.

She rehearsed, wrapped and stamped show bills to be sent ahead, made out tickets for the next day, typed parts from the master script, and helped sweep out the auditorium. She made all of my wardrobe and most of her own, transposed music for the actors, helped me learn my lines, tutored me in reading, writing, and arithmetic, and played the tenor sax.

One year we had a man and wife team named Clint and Gladys Cole on board. A picture taken around 1926 shows Mother and

Josephine in full plumage

Josephine and Billy
as Mehitable Cartright
and Sample Swichel
in *Ten Nights in a
Barroom*

Gladys, both with saxophones. With their marcelled hair, Kewpie lips, and Roaring Twenties dresses, they looked exactly like Tony Curtis and Jack Lemmon as Josephine and Daphne in *Some Like it Hot.*

Before the season opened, mother cleaned all the staterooms, made up the beds, and made sure that everything was in order for the actors. In the spring, before the cook came on board, and in the fall, after he left, she prepared meals like a gourmet chef. As showboaters go, mother was practically perfect. If she had a flaw, it was a minor one and totally beyond her control.

Through absolutely no fault of her own, mother was born with an overactive pitch-it-to-'em-ary gland, and handling concessions gave her more pleasure than any other facet of showboat life. She always had cloth bags of change hanging on coat hangers in the closet, stuffed under the mattress, and buried in drawers. She was never more happy than when she was sitting cross-legged in the middle of her big bed, counting, sorting, and rolling coins into little paper-covered

Josephine Bryant
and
Gladys Cole

logs. Sometimes I would sit and help her, making huge piles of dimes, nickles, pennies, and quarters all over the feather-tick that covered the bed. As we sorted and rolled, she would tell me of some of her early escapades in the world of commerce. As a child of nine in Logansport, Indiana, she went from house to house selling magazine subscriptions for a chance to win a Shetland pony. Then she sold embroidery thread, followed by boxes of soap.

She really hit her stride when a drummer, or door-to-door salesman, offered her "an opportunity to go into business for yourself, little lady, by helping us introduce this dee-lightful, hygee-nic, and ree-juvinating new product in your neighborhood." Mother's

Postcards Betty sold after shows

imitation of this smooth-talking character was so perfect I could easily see why she had the screen door unlocked and the carton in her hand and was halfway around the block selling chewing gum before you could say, "I want my money back."

She sold the gum for four cents a package and by the end of the day was out of stock. She sat at the kitchen table and counted her money. One dollar and ninety-four cents plus forty-eight cents in her piggy bank gave her two dollars and forty cents. A princely sum.

The man never returned, so after a reasonably ethical length of time, mother clipped an ad out of a Chicago newspaper and invested half of her capital in twenty-four pieces of white cloth, each a foot square. They were represented as having been treated with an ice-preserving chemical and when placed on top of a chunk of ice in your icebox were guaranteed to slow the melting process down by 25 percent. The cloth squares arrived and Mother sold them all in two days. However, within a week the doorbell began to ring con-

stantly as dissatisfied customers came to demand refunds. Mother's career in sales came to an abrupt end.

When mother joined the showboat, she thought she was just going to play the piano. But of all the surprises in store for her, the endless opportunities to sell concessions were the most exciting. When the boats closed in the fall, she would send away for different products to sell, and then she would canvass door to door. At that point she certainly didn't need the money, but it seemed to be a compulsion. She sold ladies' turbans and demonstrated how to wrap and tie them. She sold little clay pigs with mysteriously wiggling eyes, ears, and tails, reversible felt hats in two colors that could be worn nine different ways, and one year she sold milk bottle cap-removers.

In those days, milk was sold in glass bottles with round cardboard disks for caps. The caps fitted snugly into the neck of the bottle and had no tabs to pull them out by. It wasn't often that you could get the cap off without splashing milk all over the table. Mother's Easy Cap-Remover solved the problem. It was an aluminum cover which fitted over the top of the bottle. On the underside, two pointed pieces of metal protruded from the middle out toward each edge. By pressing the remover on the cardboard cap and twisting it, one could lift the lid without a struggle.

One year she couldn't find a product she liked so she made and sold butterflies. A large double-set of crepe-paper wings were gathered into the prongs of an old-style peg clothespin. The clothespin was then painted gold. Felt-covered wire was twisted around one end, and two sequins were glued on for eyes. With a wide stripe of gold edging and two large dots on each wing, they were ready to sell at twenty-five cents a piece.

Suffering from such an affliction, Mother could hardly be blamed for seeing me, with my ability to make change at a tender age, as a valuable employee. She had me selling candy by the time I was six years old, peddling it out of a specially built miniature tray. I sold popcorn from a basket and chewing gum and Cracker Jack from a box. My sales record was phenomenal. It's hard to resist a six-year-old huckster with a big smile.

After I had pitched everything we had to offer between acts, as the final curtain came down I would hurry around the outside guard and station myself on a little platform placed just inside the exit. I wore a little smock that sported two huge pockets for change, and as the people filed out, I stood, waving pictures of me and the showboat in the air hollering, "Souvenir postcards! Five cents each, six for a quarter! Souvenir postcards! Five cents each, six for a quarter!"

That was Mother!

THEN THERE WAS DAD

In all of his writings, speaking engagements, and interviews, Dad invariably credited his parents with the success of the *Bryant's Showboat*. It is true that, in the beginning, their fortitude, diligence, and courage was what kept the family together and on the road to success. Sam built their first little houseboat as well as the *Princess*, and Violet kept him on course and supported the family while they realized their dreams. But, once *Bryant's New Showboat* was launched, Dad immediately became the driving force behind its operation.

He was co-owner, general manager, producer, and captain. Everyone called my grandfather Captain Sam, but it was merely a token of respect. When they called Dad Captain Billy it was because, like Mark Twain, he had studied the rivers and earned the title. He held captain's papers from the head of the Allegheny to the lower Mississippi.

Dad made all the business arrangements, did the hiring and firing, laid out the route, handled publicity, and piloted the boats. He shopped for supplies, picked up the mail, paid for all license and wharf fees, and bought and arranged for delivery of coal.

A coal barge would tie up to the *Valley Belle*, and narrow planks would be laid up and over the gunnels. Every able-bodied man who wasn't an actor would man wheel-barrows and shovels to load the coal on board. It was paid for by the bushel on an estimate of two bushels to a barrow load.

(*Left to right*) Richard Costello (Betty's maternal grandfather), Billy, and a deckhand

Coaling up

Dad also directed the shows, wrote some of them, and doctored others. He played a part in every play, conducted the candy sale, and led the audience in community singing with such songs as "In the Good Old Summertime," "In the Shade of the Old Apple Tree," "School Days," and "I Want a Girl Just Like the Girl That Married Dear Old Dad." The songs were illustrated by colored slides which were projected onto a white curtain from a stereopticon in the balcony. He also did specialties. He sang, did monologues, and danced the sand dance, chair dance, soft-shoe, and buck and wing.

Buck and wing was the forerunner of modern tap dancing. A combination of the Schottische and Irish jig, it also incorporated some of the clacking steps of Flemish folk dancing and the Spanish flamenco. It was performed in low-cut shoes with leather tops attached to solid wooden soles. Eventually, a modified version of the shoe with a heel and half-sole of wood sewn to a conventional leather sole was known as split shank.

Dad's day began before sunup. He would get up, get dressed, go to the galley for his first cup of coffee, and then climb the ladder to the pilot house on the showboat. He would give the orders to cast off and would pilot the boats to the next town, usually about a two-hour trip.

When the boats were landed, he would indicate the route for the path up the bank and set the crew to building it. Then, after seeing that the auditorium was being swept up from the previous night's performance and making sure everything was in order in the ticket office, he would go up the hill and walk to the store, where he would buy supplies and ask for the mail. A deckhand or the cabin boy always went along to help carry the groceries.

A couple of passes to the show for the owner of the store was an expected gesture. In return, the best cuts of meat were brought out. Suet and soup bones were always free, and livers, hearts, and kidneys sold at ten cents a pound.

After sending the boy back to the boat with his purchases, Dad would give the postmaster a pair of free tickets and then go to the newspaper to pay two dollars for the ad that had been mailed in. After that, he would go to see the city clerk at the courthouse and buy a license to use the landing.

Depending on the size of the town, the license would run anywhere from two to twenty dollars. If it was any higher than that, Dad would merely move the boats the very short distance to the city limits. He would have a path cut through the willows to the top of the bank and tell Mother to play the calliope every two hours all day long.

Sometimes, if there was a ferry boat in town, Dad would tie up on the opposite side of the river. Then he would approach the ferry boat owner, who normally closed down around eight. Dad would give him five dollars and enough passes for his family. The ferry boat would remain in operation long enough after the show to carry the entire audience back across the river.

Leaving the city hall, Dad would return to the boat in time for midday dinner, after which he would take a well-deserved nap. When he woke, around two, he would select and prepare show bills for the towns farther down river. On the bottom of each sheet he would paint the town's name and the date of our appearance. Then he would give them to mother to bundle and wrap for mailing. He would write letters and spend an hour or two working on his autobiography and on original plays and songs. After supper, Dad, like everyone else on board, would get ready for the evening's performance. At fifteen minutes before curtain time he would go backstage to make sure everyone was accounted for.

The parts Dad played were usually comic, Toby's, silly kids, and blackface characters. They were always sympathetic and often saved the day in the last act. He usually wore a variety of odd hats, homespun shirts, and moderately baggy pants, except in the wedding scene in *Ten Nights in a Barroom*, for which he wore a pair of too-short pants with legs tight enough to inspire the line, "These pants ain't too tight, I'm just too far in 'em."

After the first act, he would come out "in one." Strolling on stage, he would walk up to one of the buildings painted on the curtain and peer into a third-floor window. Then he would turn to the audience and say, "There's a sewing machine running up and down in there without a stitch on it!" From then on, he could do no wrong.

He would begin his specialty with a monologue.

"My but it's nice to be back in Sistersville and to see all of you good people again. I remember every single one of you from our last trip." The crowd would titter. "Oh yes I do! I've got a great memory. You wouldn't believe how far back I can remember! Why, I can remember the first day I was born. I remember it just like it was yesterday.

"When I was born there was three of us, George, Henry, myself, and me. Four of us? No, three. We were all layin' in a cradle. I remember it was a cradle 'cause I was always telling my brother George to move over.

"Father came home at four-thirty in the afternoon. I know it was four-thirty 'cause I looked at the clock just before he came in. He came over and he picked me out of the cradle and he bounced me up and down in the air and he said, 'Boo BOO Boo!' I didn't say anything. I never did talk back to the old man. So, he bounced me up again. He said, 'Boo BOO boo!' I never said anything so he bounced me up again saying, 'Boo BOO boo!' Finally, I had to tell him to cut it out. I was getting dizzy.

"Pa went into the next room where Ma was. We could hear them talking. He said, 'Ma, that's the cutest bunch of snookums in there I've ever seen. Now, you go in and pick out the one you want and I'll take the rest out somewhere and drown 'em.' That made my brother George mad. He wouldn't speak to Dad for a week.

"I was the cutest baby when I was first born. And smart? Why, I had my eyes open the first day I was born! What do you think of that? And breathing! Just like a human being! I could feel the seewee-dees on my little chest going up and down. And cute? People used to come for miles around to see me. They came from France, Germany, England, Wales, jails! And the cities too! They came from Paris, London, Rome [local small town].

"My brother and I looked exactly alike. Nobody could tell us apart. The only difference was I had two teeth and he didn't have any. The only way mother could tell us apart was she'd stick her finger in George's mouth and if he'd bite her, it would be me.

"We had an awful big family. There was twenty-three children in our family, or was it twenty-four? They came along so fast one year I lost track of 'em. I always had to eat at the second table. I was twelve years old before I knew a chicken had anything but a neck.

"We were a religious family. Every Sunday Dad would hitch up the four-wheeled horse and the bobbed-tail buggy and those twenty-four children would climb in and we'd drive to church. My, but that buggy was crowded. I had to sit in the whip-socket.

"One Sunday, Dad hitched up the horse and drove to church. That old horse ran away thirteen times between the house and the church. All the way there, Dad kept hollering, 'WHOA NANCY!'

"By the time we got to church, he was so worn out, he sat down and went right to sleep. By and by, a heavyset lady came into church and sat right down next to Dad. Every time the minister would say something, she'd holler, 'AMEN!' and nudge the old man in the ribs. Dad was still asleep and he'd yell, 'WHOA NANCY!'

"Pretty soon the minister said something the lady really liked. She jumped up in the air and come down right in the old man's lap. He grabbed her around the waist, nudged me in the ribs, and yelled, 'Get up quick! Cut loose the traces and undo the britches! The old mare's gonna kick the dashboard over'"

At the piano, in the orchestra pit, Mother would burst into the introduction to a song, "Music with My Meals," "I'm Gettin' Awful Lazy," or my favorite, "The Boarder Song":

(Verse)
I'm as happy as I can be,
No more working in the factory.
I'm gettin' healthy, I'm gettin' wealthy,
Since we've added to the family.
He's a boarder and he's here to stay.
My wife rented him a room one day.
He's a staker for the butcher and the baker
That's the reason why I say,

(Chorus)
We've got a boarder, a nice young boarder.
He's such a pal to me.
When I'm not about, he always helps my wifie out.
He sweeps up, and keeps up, our whole family,
God Bless Him!
He bought my wifie a brand new shirtwaist.
It fit her perfectly.
He's so clever and so wise,
He even knew her proper size!
That boarder is certainly good to me!

Then Dad would do a buck dance to the first half of the second
chorus and pick up the lyrics on the bridge.

Last night, I came home a little early,
She was perched upon his knee.
They think they've laid me on the shelf,
But I was a boarder once myself.
That boarder is certainly good to me!

Dad would exit but in answer to tumultuous applause, he would
return to sing one of his own compositions: "I'm Glad I'm a Rube
from the Farm," "In the Days of the Govener's Son," or "Arkansas."
After that he would continue as his character in the play. Song slides
and the candy sale occupied him after the second act, and then he
would finish his part in the third act.

Often, after the show, when mother was playing the chaser
music for the people to leave by, they just would not go! Children

Billy Bryant

would dance in the aisles and adults would simply sit, loathe to return to reality. Then Dad would once again come on stage and Mother would play softly as he spoke. "Well, folks, that's it for tonight. You've been a wonderful audience, and we all thank you from the bottom of our hearts. We have to go now—folks are waiting for us downriver—but we'll be thinking of all of you, and, if God's willing and the creeks don't rise, we'll see you all again, come next showboat time." Then he would make his way to the front deck where he would stand, shaking hands and bidding people good night.

Dad was always in complete control of every situation. From the pilot house he could tell in an instant if there was trouble in the engine room, just by an unusual shudder in the boat or a slight irregularity in the sound of the wheel buckets hitting the water.

If, in the dead of night, the river took a sudden drop, or a quickening breeze and a silent streak of lightning hinted of an impending storm, some deep-rooted instinct would pull him from a sound sleep and send him out on deck in long johns and a hat, issuing orders to "Trip that spar! Tighten that headline! Get up steam!"

He had an equally uncanny ability to read the thoughts of people, especially Mother, Sam, and Violet.

Like all actors of that era, each member of the family wore a grouch bag. A grouch bag was a little cloth envelope in which performers kept their money. Men wore them on strings around their necks and women pinned them to their undergarments. The name is said to come from the actor's desire to have ready exit money in case the boss proved to be a grouch. Violet wore hers pinned to the top of her corset. It was hand-crocheted, and she spent the entire summer scrounging money to fill it.

No member of the family received a salary as such, but Mother and Lady Violet divided the concessions. Violet had the X, or exclusive, on peanuts ("'ot, fresh-roasted hin the shell"), Mother had the popcorn, and between them they split equally the profits from the sale of prize candy. The candy sold for ten cents a box, with actors,

Betty selling
tickets

family and crew members acting as candy butchers on a 10 percent
commission. We carried trays that held fifty boxes, and it was not
unusual for an excited customer to buy the whole lot at one time.

In addition to this major and lucrative source of income, there
was an established and accepted pattern of small-time pilfering that
the family members carried on at the cash drawer. The box office,
with a window cut through the wall to the front porch, was opposite our living quarters. Mother and I sold tickets off and on all
throughout the day. The show started at eight o'clock. By about
seven o'clock people began to form a line outside the window.

Usually, Dad would sell tickets for the first twenty minutes
while Mother was putting on her makeup. She would take over at
about seven-twenty. About 7:35 Violet would come in while Mother

and I went backstage to play the overture. Sam would relieve Violet
at five of eight and stay in the box office until the last minute.

Just before the curtain went up, when the border lights on stage
were flashed as a cue that the show was about to start, Sam would
close the ticket window and dash around the guard for his entrance,
leaving a deckhand on the door to pick up any stray change from
latecomers.

It was understood, though never mentioned, that, (except for
me), whoever was selling tickets would automatically pocket from
twenty-five cents to two dollars, depending on how good business
was during the shift.

After the show, I would sit with Dad at his desk in the office
while, by the light of a coal-oil lamp, he made entries in a big gray
ledger. One page was headed TICKETS, the other, NUT. He would
write the date on the top of each page and the list, under TICKETS:

102 Gen. Adm.	.25¢	-	$ 25.50
176 Balc.	.50¢	-	88.00
198 Resvd.	.75¢	-	269.00
		GROSS	$382.50

Then, under NUT:

Groceries	-	$12.95
Coal	-	75.00
License fee	-	2.00
Sam	-	.25
Violet	-	.75
Josie	-	1.50

I never found out how he knew who took what, but he knew.
Furthermore, he approved. He wanted them to have the money, but
the rule of "steal it" was absolute.

One day mother told him she needed a dollar for something or
other and he said, offhandedly, "Take it out of the drawer."

That night, during Dad's shift at the ticket window, Mother reached around him and picked out a dollar from the drawer.

"What do you think you're doing?" he yelled.

"You told me today to take a dollar out of the drawer," she said.

"Well, dammit!" he screamed, his face turning a deep purple, "TAKE IT WHEN I'M NOT LOOKING!"

Occasionally, Violet ran into a conflict between art and finance, but she took the hurdle in stride. Two of her favorite shows were *Over the Hill to the Poorhouse* and *At the End of the Road*. Her part in each play was a thespian plum fit to serve to a Barrymore. She was onstage from the moment the curtain rose till it fell at the end of the last act, and she reveled in the roles.

However, getting ready for the parts took time and involved carefully settling a white wig over her hennaed hair, drawing heavy lines into her wrinkle-remover-saturated skin, and transforming her appearance in general to her real age, which she so diligently and successfully labored to conceal. The ritual completely eliminated her as ticket seller for the run of that play, and she was constantly torn between her love for those parts and the devastating diet they imposed on her grouch bag.

Her solution to the problem aged me beyond my years. Obviously, it's impractical to carry silver in a grouch bag, and the larger the denomination of bills, the smaller the bulge. On this premise, Violet would wait until I was in the box office. Then she would send down a deckhand, who was acting as an usher, with a lace handkerchief wrapped around four dollars and twenty-five cents worth of change. Pinned to it was a note: "Will you please give me a five dollar bill for this?"

The first time it happened, I was so frightened at being an unwilling accomplice that I could hardly remember my lines on stage and I dreaded to see the evening end. I felt sure that Dad would somehow be made aware of my duplicity and accuse me of, at the very least, petty theft.

The show ended, the crowd went home, and the generator was turned off. Dad was settled at his desk, and I sat on the prop trunk by his side. I chewed on my lower lip as he opened the gray book, turned to a fresh sheet and dipped his pen in the ink.

He entered the amounts of tickets sold and then, without pause, went to the other side and recorded,

Groceries	-	$13.50
License fee	-	2.50
Sam	-	.50
Josie	-	1.00
Violet	-	.75

That was my dad.

PHONE IT IN

After Moscow, we would play New Richmond, Ohio. Then we would steam past Cincinnati without a second thought, never dreaming what a great part the Queen City was to play in our lives.

Each season we traveled the same route, but occasionally we would add a town or two. Sometimes, we passed up a regular stop because of unusual circumstances, such as weather conditions, flooding, or quarantine. In October of 1918, during the terrible flu epidemic, Mother lost a brother and a sister within three days of each other. When she went home, a newspaper reported it: "Mrs. Billy Bryant, wife of Billy Bryant, manager of Bryant's Showboat, was called home last week to Logansport, Indiana on account of the sickness of her brother and sister Richard and Mary Costello, four and sixteen years old, respectively. Both died of influenza at their home in Logansport, Indiana, October 25. The Bryant's Showboat is laid up at present at Gallatin, Pennsylvania, with the 'flue' all around it."

The first towns in Indiana we stopped at were Greendale, Aurora, and Rising Sun, across the river from Rabbit Hash, Kentucky. We used to ferry people from Rabbit Hash to see the show. One of them explained the name of their town.

It seems that almost two hundred years ago, when it was just a nameless pioneer settlement, one of the residents was complaining that all he would have for Thanksgiving dinner was rabbit hash, an

Indian mixture of bird, squirrel, and rabbit meat. The other settlers were so amused they decided to name the little settlement "Rabbit Hash."

By now, we were deep in the Ohio Valley, and the towns we played rarely boasted a population of more than six hundred. Our arrival was a signal for a spontaneous holiday and often farmers, in their anxiety to buy tickets, would row out in johnboats to meet us in midstream. All day long they came on board to buy tickets, visit, and show off new babies. Often they brought gifts, armloads of wet lilacs, roses, peonies, homemade preserves, a bit of tatting, a sampler, a glass of quince jelly, or a freshly baked pie. They greeted us as old friends and were anxious for news from up or down river.

The price of admission was fifty cents for a reserved seat, thirty-five for general admission, and twenty-five for children. But in the valley, farmers often came in with something to swap and a sad story about children being more plentiful than money. It wasn't unusual for us to play to a half-cash house and a box office filled with chickens, eggs, hams, and baskets of grapes or buckets of berries.

Sometimes, we would nose the boats right into a clump of willows to tie up at a place too small to be called more than "Somebody's Landing." The deckhands would hack a path to the top of the hill where the only sign of life might be a sad-eyed cow grazing at the edge of a plowed field. The hands would dig deep steps into the dirt and sprinkle them with sawdust. Then Mother would go up top for the calliope concert, and the strains of *Let Me Call You Sweetheart"* would echo out over the fields and through the hills.

All day long we'd meet no one, but by sundown, as far as the eye could see from the top of the showboat, the dusty dirt roads that bordered the fields would be lined with jolting wagons filled with people who laughed and sang. Occasionally, a happy barefoot boy would ride up on a weary old mule, heeling him in the sides and urging him on with "Come on, Sassafras! We're going to the showboat!"

Contrary to the legend that has sprung up, river audiences did not, originally, cheer the hero and hiss the villain. When thoroughly enthused, they would whistle and stamp their feet, but otherwise they became completely absorbed in the plot. They cursed the villain beneath their breath, mumbled encouragement to the hero, and shed unabashed tears when Little Eva died and went to heaven. Women sat with bated breath, clinging to their escorts' arms when the leading lady was threatened, and more than one actor, while playing a particularly nasty part, has been tossed overboard by some gallant member of the audience who took it upon himself to right the wrong he saw on stage.

Audiences preferred old-fashioned melodramas with plenty of tears and laughter, and they would not tolerate intermissions. If the show lasted less than two hours, they felt cheated, and, above all, the plays had to be scrupulously clean. It was even better if they delivered a message. *Ten Nights in a Barroom* deplored the evils of Demon Rum. *Uncle Tom's Cabin* decried the disgrace of slavery, and *East Lynne* verbally wagged a castigating finger at adultery.

In each of these plays the child star died at the end of the second act. On a cot, surrounded by his or her family, the child would hold forth eloquently and interminably on the evils of the world, breathing a last breath only after securing a promise from loved ones that these things would be changed.

The last scene in the play was called "The Transformation." It showed the effects of the child's death on the survivors. Reformed, respected, and obviously prospering, everyone stood around speaking of the child and telling each other how fortunate they were to have heeded his or her warning. Suddenly, the cast would freeze, in tableau, like living statues, as the lights grew dim and soft music began to play. Then a baby-spot would light the center of the backdrop, and the audience would gasp as an angel appeared.

Standing behind a filmy curtain on a soap box covered with a sheet, the child wore a long, white nightgown and cheesecloth wings. A halo made of wire wrapped in Christmas tree tinsel bobbed over the head, and the eyes, deep-set in a face liberally powdered with corn-starch, were raised heavenward. As the music swelled and the front roll curtain descended slowly, the women in the audience could be heard sobbing, and now and then a man would blow his nose. On the showboat, the transformation scene was surefire.

Considering how deeply involved the audience became with the play, it was always surprising to see how flexible and tolerant they could be in cases of emergency. A sudden illness causing a change in the cast or an unavoidable interruption by something happening in the audience was taken in good humor, and as soon as the problem was solved they would immediately go back into their near hypnotic state.

Playing, as we did, tiny villages and landings, it was often easier to find a horse doctor than a general practitioner, and much of our medicine came from the kitchen. Mother firmly believed that if something couldn't be cured by salt, vinegar, or baking soda, it was terminal, and she had first-aid kits with these three ingredients stashed all over the boats.

Mild saltwater was used for, among other things, minor wounds, canker sores, or a clogged sinus. Baking soda soothed insect bites, fever, pulled muscles, or upset stomachs, and plain red vinegar was applied both in- and ex-ternally for maladies too numerous to mention.

Fortunately, showboating was basically an extremely healthful lifestyle. Plenty of sleep in a room filled with fresh, cool breezes, wholesome meals served at regular hours, and constant opportunities for practically irresistible exercise in the form of a walk down a country lane or an invigorating swim across the still unpolluted river.

Occasionally, we had an accident on board, usually involving a member of the crew or family and occurring during the moving of the boats. At one point, my grandfather was caught in a vicious coil of wire cable that parted in a storm and wrapped itself around his legs like the line that entrapped the fisherman in *Captains Courageous*. He was taken to the nearest hospital by packet boat.

Another time, Leo was badly injured while trying to free the stern wheel of piled-up driftwood. The current turned the paddle wheel and brought the cam down on Leo's shoulder. Fortunately we were tied up just outside a major city and were able to rush him to the landing in a motorboat and from there by ambulance to the hospital.

The actors were rarely sick. When they were, the audience was seldom aware of it. I can't remember ever actually hearing the phrase "the show must go on," but it was an assumed fact of life, and no aggregation of actors in the history of the theater has ever been more proficient at the art of "phoning it in" than a troupe of showboat performers.

If an actor suddenly became indisposed, when it was time for him to appear, the phone would ring. One of the actors, already on stage, would answer it and deliver the ailing thespian's lines as though he were repeating what was being said on the phone.

Thus, a scene for an old melodrama as performed with Dave, a main character, missing:

(HELEN AND WALLACE DISCOVERED ON STAGE)
> Helen

Wallace, it's nearly midnight and Dave is not yet here! We can not wait much longer!
> Wallace

Never fear, Helen, Dave will not fail. He promised to be back with the proof that our father is innocent and he WILL be here! (PHONE RINGS. WALLACE ANSWERS IT) Hello, Dave? (TO HELEN) It's Dave. (INTO PHONE) Where are you, Dave? (PAUSE. TO HELEN) He's at the farm. (INTO PHONE) Did you get it? (TO HELEN) He has it! (INTO PHONE) Are you bringing it here? (PAUSE) No? Then where? (PAUSE) What time? (PAUSE) All right, Dave. Good work lad, good work! (HANGS UP PHONE. CROSS TO HELEN) Dave has all the proof we need. He's bringing it to the Old Mill. I'll meet him there and take it to the Court House in the morning. You see, Helen, I told you Dave would not fail! (EMBRACE. CURTAIN)

All the actors knew all of the lines in all of the plays, so the ruse worked very well. It did, that is, until one summer when we were playing *Agnes, the Switchman's Daughter*.

For minor, bit parts, Dad often called on members of the crew. One of the funniest and most willing we ever had was an engineer called Shorty. Shorty was with us for many years, and he was quite accustomed to playing "supers" (characters with no lines to speak), such as policemen, gangsters, and cowboys. He was not exactly a quick study, so his occasional rhetoric was limited to lines like, "Put up your hands!", "Oh, no you don't!" or "Get over there!" Then, one night, at Warsaw, Ohio, Thespis took Shorty by the hand and led him down the path to where stars are born.

It was the end of the second act. The set was an interior. Shorty, as the villain's henchman, was holding the switchman at gunpoint, preventing him from running to save his daughter, Agnes, who was tied to the railroad tracks, offstage.

The leading man was due to enter behind Shorty, take in the situation, and hit him over the head. Unfortunately, Doug Morris the leading man, was totally occupied being very ill over the outside guardrail. Dad rushed to the wings on the side of the stage nearest to Shorty, who was standing perplexed about what to do with his captive. The character man, in the role of the switchman, was ad libbing wildly about his daughter, the approaching train, and so forth.

In a loud, hoarse whisper, Dad informed Shorty, "We're phoning him in!"

At that moment, the phone rang on stage. Shorty went to the table. Shifting the gun to his left hand, he lifted the receiver to his ear and said, "Hello. Who? John Caldwell? What's that you say? *Put up my hands?*" With that, he laid the gun on the table and raised his hands high above his head.

The switchman beat a hasty retreat and the curtain rolled down to a roaring mixture of cheers and applause.

VIC FAUST

Some of the showboat impresarios played the show straight through and then followed it with an olio of vaudeville. My father preferred to give the audience time to dry their tears by putting the vaudeville in between the acts.

All of the actors did specialties. Perhaps the villain, standing in front of illustrated lantern slides, would warble "She's Only a Bird in a Gilded Cage," or the leading lady might render her version of "After the Ball Was Over." Man and wife teams would sometimes dance, play musical instruments or do tumbling. Graham and Golden did a clever racetrack bit with original patter and finished with an eccentric dance. One actor juggled Indian clubs while riding a unicycle. Most of the men could sing and do character readings or impersonations, and it was not unusual for the character man to don a cutaway coat and a stovepipe hat to deliver a stump speech.

In those days, itinerant preachers who traveled the hills and valleys by horseback gave their sermons while standing behind a waist-high tree stump. They would add force to their oratory by striking the top of the stump with a cane or a rolled up newspaper each time they felt compelled to accentuate a point.

Actors who did stump speeches parodied these preachers, delivering a comic monologue from behind a prop stump. In high camp, they would whack the top of the stump with a dilapidated, folded umbrella each time they came to the punch line of a joke.

Vic Faust

A typical and extremely popular showboat performer was a man by the name of Vic Faust. Vic was a versatile entertainer from Australia. He had played some of the finest theaters in the world, but after one season on a showboat he found himself totally captivated by a lifestyle that allowed him to combine his two great loves, entertaining and fishing. He was with us for years and created quite a following for himself among the river audiences.

Vic worked in "rube" wardrobe, *rube* being a term applied to farmers, many of whom bore the name of Reuben. His makeup consisted of wire-rimmed spectacles, jutting chin whiskers, and a bright red wig of hemp which stuck out from his head at all angles.

The skintightness of his too-short trousers was accentuated by his suspender-wrinkled shirt and grotesque slap shoes which buttoned up over his ankles and stuck out in front of him like the feet of a well-shod duck.

Vic played, among other things, the violin, a musical saw, chimes, and a one-string fiddle. He also coaxed melodies out of children's toys, whistles with sliding handles, leaking balloons, and a tiny xylophone. The xylophone was mounted on an artist's easel in front of a landscape painting, which gave it the appearance of a railroad track that was fading in the distance.

As the front curtain was rolled up, the piano player struck up a bouncy, lilting melody that had the audience grinning and tapping their toes. Vic would walk to the center of the stage, strutting like a peahen. Then, in a voice to match his costume, he would start to sing,

> How'd do, how be you?
> Mighty pleased to meet you, too.
> My name is Josh-away
> Ebeneezer Spry.
> I know a thing or two,
> You bet your life I do.
> You can't fool me
> 'Cause I'm too durn sly.

> I swan, I must be gettin' on.
> Giddy-up Napoleon
> It looks like rain.
> I'll be switched,
> The hay ain't pitched,
> Come in when you're over
> To the farm again.

The music would vamp while he strutted in a little circle. Then he would start again.

> I've met Bunko men
> Always got the best of them.
> One said, "Give me two tens fer a five."
> I said, "that'll do"
> I be the constabule.
> Now you're arrested
> As sure as you're alive."

> I swan, I must be gettin' on. . . .

By now the crowd was clapping their hands in time to the music and joining in on the chorus, and when he made one more little strutting circle at the end, he did it to the accompaniment of cheers and applause.

When the audience had quieted down, Vic would walk to the side of the stage, reach through the curtain, and bring out a chair and his one-string fiddle and bow. Carrying the instrument in one hand, he would drag the chair to the center of the stage with the other, sit down, and tune his fiddle, keeping his eyes on the people all the while.

The fiddle was made of a cigar box with a hole cut in the lid. From one end, a sawed-off broom handle protruded. In the tip of the handle, a wooden peg held one end of a violin string that was stretched to the bottom of the cigar box.

Satisfied with his tuning, Vic would place the box between his knees, holding the broom handle like the neck of a cello. Then he would nod to the piano player and, with his eyes roving along the first row of seats, play "Let Me Call You Sweetheart, I'm in Love With You."

He always timed his first pause so he would be looking at a pretty young girl. Then he would roll his eyes and grin like a Cheshire cat, exposing, for the first time, a dark hole that had once housed two now-missing front teeth. Turning a bright red, the girl would collapse in a flood of embarrassed giggles.

For the rest of the song, Vic never took his eyes off her, and, by the time he hit the finishing high note and gave her one last smile, she was usually sitting with her head in her lap, her hands covering her face, and her shoulders shaking in uncontrollable gales of laughter.

His final offering was an exhibition of Swiss bell ringing. Two wooden handles, much like those on a jump rope, were bolted to a small metal frame eight inches square. Attached to the frame, with the open ends up, were four bells, each about six inches deep.

The bells were tuned, and, by tilting the handles this way and that, Vic produced lovely, melodious tunes like "When Irish Eyes Are Smiling" and "The World Is Waiting For the Sunrise."

For his closing number Vic played two choruses of a rousing and effective arrangement of "The Bells of Saint Mary's" and, with a final grin at the still giggling young girl, retired to a thunderous roar of applause.

Removing his wig and whiskers, he walked to the stern of the boat to get back to serious fishing, satisfied that he had, as always, pleased everyone, including the captain. Once again, he had given the perfect performance by all showboat standards: he had been funny, clever, and clean.

After Warsaw, Kentucky, we played Vevay, Ohio. At Carrolton, Kentucky, we turned off the Ohio to go up the Kentucky River, past the Twin Chimneys, Brooklyn, Gilberts Creek, and Dix River. The two weeks we spent each year going up and down that beautiful stream was a delight to all of us. But for Vic Faust the time spent on the Kentucky River with its little side creeks and hidden pools filled to capacity with ever-hungry mountain bass, blue gill, and crappy was like an annual visit to paradise.

Every morning, as soon as the gangplank was out, Vic was on the bank, pole and bait can in hand, striding off on his eternal quest for the big ones. If that wasn't enough to runneth his cup over, one year there was Polly.

Polly was an Irish biddy of a cook who had a brogue thick enough to sole a boot. With her hair tucked into a mobcap and an all-encompassing apron tied about her ample middle, Polly ruled the kitchen with an iron hand encased in a velvet glove. Meals were served on time and people who arrived late risked her wrath in the form of a vehement tongue-lashing. However, if anyone on board fell sick or came down with the "miseries," chicken broth and cup custard would appear like magic on the nightstand in his stateroom.

A request of special dishes would be met with, "Sure, and where do you think you are—at the Waldorf Astoria?" But Polly took an instant liking to Vic, and, having a wonderful way with fish, she went to great lengths to prepare any and everything he brought on board.

Vic was forever dragging in enormous strings of shiners, or sunfish. After cutting off the head and tail, all that was left was a bit no bigger than a silver dollar. It took a dozen of them to make a man-sized meal, but if properly pan fried, they were as sweet as a nut. Polly browned them to perfection by the skilletful.

Once on the Ohio, Vic brought in an eel. Polly skinned it, cut it into thick sections and boiled it with onions and potatoes. Another time he returned with a turtle, and, after turning it over to the deckhand for butchering and cleaning, Polly transformed it into a kettleful of delicious turtle soup.

But finally, Vic went too far. He had decided to start crawdadding, planning to use the tails for fish bait. But when, on his first time out, he caught some crawfish as big as Florida lobsters, he thought that surely Polly, with her culinary magic, could make something edible if not downright delectable out of them.

With great anticipation, he marched back to the kitchen, carrying a bucket full of the ugly crustaceans. Polly was standing on the back porch, wiping the perspiration from her brow, taking a bit of air.

Vic walked up to her. With a minimum of greeting, he pulled from the bucket one of the largest of the clawing, waving crawdads. Polly took one giant step to the rear, drew herself up, placed her hands on her broad hips and glared at Vic. "Mr. Faust," she said. "Oi've always considered meself to be a reasonable woman. Oi've fried yer minnies, oi've boiled yer sea monsters, and oi've stewed yer terrapins, but I'll be *damned* if oi'll cook that *bug!*"

Back on the Ohio we played the Indian towns of Madison, Bethlehem and New Albany. Skirting the city of Louisville, we stopped at Jeffersonville, Indiana, then on to Shively, Kentucky; New Boston, Indiana; and Rome, Indiana. The trips between towns were longer in this stretch of the river. Sometimes we would break our jump (theatrical jargon for "trip") on weekends by going halfway on Sunday and pulling in to tie up just anywhere at sundown.

On one such Sunday, I had a memorable experience.

THAT OLD-TIME RELIGION

Mother came from an Irish Catholic family named Costello (pronounced Cos-low) and married into an English Protestant family named Bryant. From that day on, she never ceased brandishing her religion at the swarm of WASPs she had elected to join and was fanatical in her determination to raise me in the Catholic faith.

Along our route, Catholic churches were scarce, but occasionally a priest, like a circuit rider in frontier days, would arrive at a landing to baptize babies, bless marriages, and say Mass. On those occasions, Mother would stock up on supplies so she always would have a goodly amount of religious pictures, holy water, and candles on hand.

For one half hour each day, with the air and demeanor of an inquisitor, mother subjected me to a lesson in religion. My textbook was the Baltimore Catechism, and by the age of seven I could parrot the answers to every one of the questions in that formidable book.

Dad, on the other hand, sort of took his religion where he found it. Every Sunday evening (we never had a show on Sunday), he would get dressed in his blue serge suit, a white shirt, and a bow tie and wait while mother dressed me in a hand-embroidered crepe shift, white stockings, and black button shoes.

After Mother put on her wine-colored two-piece suit, a short strand of pearls at her throat, and a large, black straw hat decorated with silk flowers, Dad would lead us into the semi-wilderness to find a church, any church.

Sometimes, if the town were large enough, the church would turn out to be a small but pretty structure with colored glass in the windows and a traditional steeple housing a bell, which often had been salvaged from a sunken steamboat. Sometimes it would be a converted schoolhouse located in the middle of a field. Other times the church was a faded tent with a kitchen table serving as a pulpit and rough boards stretched over nail kegs for seats.

Often, we walked for miles along dusty, country roads or over open fields. I loved those evenings with Dad holding my hand or carrying me on his shoulder. Lightning bugs twinkled in the dusk while crickets sawed their serenades. The air was heavy with the smell of clover, honeysuckle, or freshly plowed earth. Mother always trotted along a few feet in the rear, tight-lipped and undoubtedly praying for forgiveness every step of the way.

One night is forever etched in my memory. I was about six years old. The boats were tied up halfway between towns. The twenty-mile jump we were making was considered long, and we planned to finish it in the morning.

Our deckhand cut a path through the willows, and up we went. At the top of the bank railroad tracks ran parallel to the river. On the other side of the tracks fields of ripe corn seemed to cover the universe, the tall, green stalks standing in symmetrical rows like soldiers on guard in the Emerald City.

Dad tossed me to his shoulder and began to follow the tracks, stepping from tie to tie and singing softly in a sweet, tenor voice,

> Shine on, shine on harvest moon
> Up in the sky . . .

Mother followed reluctantly.

I don't know how far we walked or what instinct prompted Dad to choose the direction he did. But after a while, we heard voices in the distance and soon a low, whitewashed, frame building came into view. We left the tracks and Dad put me down. Walking up to the door, we paused on the threshold as Mother adjusted her hat and Dad straightened his tie.

We could hear people inside, talking and laughing. Dad slowly opened the door. Lighted lanterns hung along the walls of the long, narrow room and wooden benches on either side were filled to capacity with black men, women, and children. A man in clerical robes was halfway down the center aisle, shaking hands with a huge man in clean but well-worn overalls. Suddenly he saw us, straightened up and, for a moment, stood like an ebony statue. Every eye in the room focused on us, and it was so quiet I could hear Mother breathing. Dad put out his hand.

"I'm Captain Billy Bryant from the *Bryant's Showboat*," he said, "and this is my wife and daughter." The preacher walked forward with quiet dignity and shook Dad's hand. Then he said, "God bless you, Cap'n Bryant, and welcome."

We were ushered to a front pew, people bumping into each other in their haste to make room for us. When we were settled, the preacher smiled and went to the pulpit to begin the services. I was sitting next to a little old woman who looked to be at least a hundred years old. She was shriveled and bent, with sparse strands of gray hair standing out at all angles from her head. A long, dark hair grew from a mole on her chin, and she was sucking on something that she had trapped under her upper lip. When I sat down, she greeted me with a toothless grin.

Most of the women held palm leaf fans, which they waved absentmindedly under their chins as they stared straight at the man in the pulpit. He acknowledged our presence as honored guests and bid us welcome. Then he got down to some serious Bible thumpin'. The preacher was a dedicated man and his denouncements of sin were delivered in awesome tones, punctuated with dramatic gestures. Slowly, he swept his parishioners with a stony stare and then cautioned them to beware of the devil's tools.

The old woman at my side swayed back and forth gently as the sermon went on. Occasionally an "A-MEN!" would erupt from somewhere in the room. As the oratory grew louder and more intense, she swayed faster and mumbled her approval at certain passages.

Near the climax of the sermon, the preacher pointed an accusative finger at his flock and ordered them to give up gambling, refrain from drinking, and "cease dallying with the whores of Babylon!"

"That's preachin', brother!" shouted the old woman. "THAT'S PREACHIN'!" And the entire congregation endorsed her shout of praise with a robust "HALLELUJAH!"

As the sermon came to a close, the people began clapping their hands. I thought for a moment they were applauding, but they were merely setting a tempo and suddenly everyone burst into song. The room was alive with men, women, and children singing and shouting praises to the Lord. Some of them stood up in the pews. Others, overcome by the spirit, rolled in the aisle, screaming and shouting, laughing and crying.

I thought it was wonderful and wished it could go on forever, but then the parson began walking down the aisle, toward the door, stopping when he came to a prone body to help the person to his or her feet. He shook hands and patted heads and kept singing at the top of his lungs.

As he passed, people left the pews and began dancing after him. I followed Mother and Dad into the aisle and when some children near me broke into a hopping, high-kicking dance, I could stand it no longer. Throwing my head back and waving my hands in the air, I cakewalked along with the best of them. I hadn't learned to mule kick on the levee for nothing!

Once the worshippers were outside, they became dramatically subdued, as though they had cast off a spell. They crowded around us and thanked us shyly for coming. Then the whole congregation disappeared into the night, and we started home down the tracks.

Mother was in a state of shock, but I was riding high on Dad's shoulder, and we sang and strutted all the way back to the boats.

From that night on, Mother doubled and redoubled her efforts to keep my feet on what she considered the right road to heaven. My religion lessons were lengthened to forty-five minutes and a prebedtime reading of bible stories was added to the curriculum.

Lord only knows she did her best, but ever since that wonderful night, to me, formal church services have somehow seemed tame.

THE SEASON ENDS

By now, summer had begun to wane. Rockport, Indiana; Owensboro, Kentucky; Evansville and Mt. Vernon, Indiana; and Uniontown, Kentucky; Elizabethtown, Illinois; Bay City, Illinois; Paducah, Kentucky; and Metropolis, Joppa, and Mound City, all in Illinois. Then we came to Cairo, Illinois, and our boats shot out into the turbulent Mississippi like a cork out of a champagne bottle. We turned upstream and the towns were even farther apart. We traveled several hours each day and bypassed some towns. Our object was to reach Alton, where we always turned off the Ohio to go up the Illinois River, which was one of the best rivers for showboats. The people loved all forms of entertainment and would sometimes follow a boat for miles to see the same performance again and again. Going upstream, we played the Illinois towns of Hardin, Kampsville, Pearl Landing, Florence, Meredosia, Beardstown, Browning, and Bath.

Between Pearl and Bath was commercial fishing country. The banks were crowded with equipment. Trotlines, traps, nets, and dozens of cane poles vied for space with the flat-bottomed boats of the musselers. The shores were covered with drying nets and pots of boiling, belching tar. Here and there a dead gar or devil dog stared with sightless eyes. Broken fish traps lay waiting for repair, and the foul odor of scalded mussels mingled with the stench of fish.

Occasionally, we would tie up nose to nose with a large, condemned wharf boat which had been turned into a fishery. Men, running trotlines or wing-nets would bring fish in by the boatload and dump them into large wooden bins. A long crude table ran down the middle of the boat, and women stood on either side, beheading and gutting each fish with three strokes of their wicked-looking knives.

The work went on well into the night, lighted by flaming torches stuck into the shallow water. At the end of the day, the women would sing as they made their way to shore over one of the long, narrow, sagging planks. They passed and greeted those who were coming to work on another plank a few feet away. Sometimes, one of the women going in to work would toss a baby across the water to another who was headed for home.

On shore, fish were sold at ten cents a pound, by estimate. A man would hold out a string of bass or catfish that reached from his shoulder to the ground, heft it a few times and say, "Fifty cents." We served a lot of fish on the Illinois.

After Bath we played Havana, Liverpool, Kingston Mines, Pekin, Lacon, and Hennepin. By then the air had grown nippy, days were shorter, and the leaves had taken on the rich bold colors of autumn. Our season had come to an end. After bidding the actors a fond adieu, we headed back to our winter quarters at West Elizabeth, Pennsylvania, on the Monongahela River.

Almost every day we traveled from sunup to sundown, but if we tied up early at any point Leo and I would be off the boat foraging for pawpaws, yellow and ripened by frost, and chestnuts, with their thick burrs split open, waiting to be taken back to the boats and roasted in a shovel over the coals in the tinder box under the boiler.

We gathered black walnuts, still in their protective green hulls, put them in a gunny sack and beat them against a flat rock with a hammer. The dark juice that soaked through would stain my fingers, and Leo said it was the same kind the Indians used to paint their faces. After the hulls had been smashed we picked out the nuts and spread them on butcher's paper in the balcony to dry.

The trip back down the Illinois and up the Ohio took between one and two weeks. Once there, the crew members, except for Leo who worked year round, went home. The family stayed on board for a few weeks. Then we would take a trip. Every other year Violet would go to England to see her relatives there. Dad would take Sam, Mother, and me to Chicago or New York.

Dad went through life with a minimum of baggage. When it came to personal belongings he hotly declared that he would never own more than he could carry. If someone gave him a new shirt or tie he would immediately dispose of an *old* shirt or tie. He carried, on the road, a brown grip, a one-suit suit bag, and a small portable typewriter. He was a redcap's nightmare.

Mother, on the other hand, traveled as lightly as a road show company of *Ben Hur*. She carried a hatbox, three suitcases, a dog carrier, a dog, a bag of needlework, a box of lunch, a fur coat, several books, an afghan, a large pillow, and her wardrobe trunk.

The trunk was dark green. On one side of it white letters spelled out JOSEPHINE BRYANT—THEATER. It stood on end and opened like a book. The right side held a rack of wooden hangers draped to capacity with mother's clothes. Underneath was a case for shoes. The case had long since been prostituted to holding miniature pots and pans, and it was always unpacked first. The cooking utensils were kept in a suitcase, under the bed, locked for insurance against prying landladies.

Meanwhile, back at the trunk, other wonders were being unfolded. The left side was built like a chest of drawers. One drawer held a sterno stove, a folding oven, and assorted bottles and cans containing butter, sugar, salt, and such. These items joined the pots and pans under the bed.

Another drawer was filled with towels, a Chinese tinkle-bell that was hung in the window (or over the door if it was a back room), and a rayon bedspread edged generously in long, intricately knotted fringe.

In the top drawer there was more fringe running around a multi-colored Spanish shawl. A framed, embroidered sampler proclaimed, in daisy-twined letters, "Home Sweet Home." Tucked neatly into a small compartment built for jewelry were six well-traveled, slightly faded artificial roses.

A satin pillow of midnight blue nestled protectively against a previously inoffensive white vase which had been painstakingly pasted over with bits of sheer, colored paper cut from the linings of Christmas card envelopes. That vase was supposed to resemble stained glass, but it looked more like a kaleidoscope that had run amok.

The pillow I considered mine. It was edged in gold fringe with an oil painting covering the top. The background was an enormous, yellow moon with a smattering of willowy leaves overlapping one edge. Against this, with a gentle breeze tossing her long hair, an equally willowy blonde was posed in yards and yards of cleverly draped chiffon. In one hand she held a leash restraining a pure white, magnificently bored Russian wolfhound. The lady's head was held high. She was smiling a sweet, gentle smile. Every time that pillow came out of the trunk I would actually choke up at the sad beauty I saw in the woman's expression.

Nevertheless, when that pillow was placed on the bed on top of the Oriental spread, and the Spanish shawl was draped over the open trunk, when the roses in their paper stained-glass vase were displayed on the dresser and the "Home Sweet Home" sampler was hung over the "No Cooking" sign, the room became, not only a home, but a monument to the kitsch taste of the twenties.

We would stay in the city for eight to ten weeks. As soon as Dad's friends knew he was in town they would call and ask him what shows we wanted to see. We saw them all.

Near the end of February we would go back to the showboat and Violet would return from England, bearing gifts. One year she brought me a beautiful baby doll with a bisque head and eyes that opened and closed. Another time, it was a little tweed skirt, a sweater, and a tam-o'-shanter to match. On every trip she brought a big log of hard candy that had a picture of the pier at Brighton running all the way through its middle.

Dad would choose scripts for the coming season and hire actors. Mother would prepare the wardrobe she would need for the opening show and order concession supplies. Sam would start to inspect every inch of the boat and begin to repair and paint anything that was not up to par. Soon the crew members and then the actors would arrive, the show would be rehearsed, and the wheel would spin once again.

SWEET BIRD OF YOUTH

Thus passed my first seven years. The summers were spent traveling up and down the Ohio and its tributaries with occasional trips up the Mississippi and the Illinois. During that time, I made countless friends who kept in touch with me for many years. I also received an invaluable education in theater that would stand me in good stead for the rest of my life.

The winters were divided between visits to New York or Chicago and a few weeks in West Elizabeth. I have many fond memories of the time we spent in that little town. In my mind, I can still see the bright stars overhead as we walked over the bridge at night to Elizabeth to see silent movies, and I can feel the cold wind as I was carried back, half-asleep on Dad's shoulder.

I can remember the nice people who had the small grocery store just a few yards back from the top of the bank where Mother would send me to buy a bottle of milk and a pie in a cardboard box. I still think of Lizzie McKinny and her son Tom, who owned a houseboat just a few yards from where we were tied up, and the Nolders family, who had the biggest German shepherd I had ever seen.

Perhaps, with the passage of time, some of these visions may fade, but the memory of what happened between Mother Violet and me during the last season we wintered there will go with me to my grave.

Josephine, Betty, and Violet Bryant on the stage plank

Violet thought "grandmother" was a word that should be spelled out in front of children, and she came to grips with the problem at an early date. I had barely begun to babble "da-da" when she gave me instructions on how she was to be addressed.

I can still remember the bewilderment I felt when a playmate, upon meeting Violet for the first time, drew me aside and whispered in awe, "Is that your grandma?" and I replied, "Oh, no. That's Mother Violet!"

I wasn't the first grandchild to muddy Violet's fountain of youth, but I was the first one fated to be permanently underfoot. My Aunt Florence had long since succumbed to the lure of city lights and for years had floated in and out of our lives sporting now a husband, now a child, now another husband, and so on. The net result was her two daughters, of whom I have only vague recollections as their visits were few and far between.

The running battle that Violet fought with age was truly herculean. There wasn't a potion, powder, liquid, or salve that could be massaged in, rubbed on, or drunk down that she didn't utilize if it so much as hinted at the promise of a delaying action in her war against the ravages of time.

Her hair was henna red and she dyed it every two weeks of her life. Every now and then, in the winter, she went to New York and had her face lifted, creeping stealthily up dark, back stairs to a doctor's dingy office where the then illegal operations were arranged for.

At the time, I didn't realize what was happening, and it was years before I understood the significance of the strategically placed false curls she wore over each temple to hide the tiny scars. Eventually, the repeated surgery took its toll. She began to have a perpetual look of surprise and gave me the uneasy feeling that she was walking on tippy toe.

A large makeup case on her dressing table was crammed with chin straps, cork plasters, tweezers, tins, bottles, and jars—all salt for the tail of the Sweet Bird of Youth. She worked diligently to keep her beauty secrets *secret* and would rather have been caught doing a walk-on in a tent show than with her hair in curlers or her face coated with cream. Still, in spite of all her precautions, when I was six years old, I saw her at the climax of her nightly cosmetic ritual, and it was an unforgettable experience.

We were getting ready for bed when Dad discovered that the alarm clock was broken. He told me to go up to Violet and Sam's room and ask to borrow theirs. My heart began to pound at the prospect. The empty cavelike auditorium was eerie at night, and Dad, with a wicked sense of humor, was not above making spooky noises to hurry me on my way. Reluctantly, I stepped out into the dark hall and quickly climbed the stairs.

Standing on the bottom step that led into their room, I knocked on the door. After a long pause, it opened slowly, revealing to my young eyes, a fearful apparition. Clothed in a flowing robe, the specter held aloft a lamp that cast an unearthly glow on its face. It had neither eyebrows nor eyelashes and was shriveled like a shrunken head, stained the color of walnuts. It began to speak, the words oozing out of the puckered lips like an unholy curse being delivered by a creature from beyond the grave.

It was more than my six-year-old courage could handle, and I staggered, screaming down the dark stairs, into our room and under the bed where I lay trembling and crying out that Mother Violet had been changed into a giant prune.

I never recovered completely from that experience, although the explanation was simple enough. Violet had merely been in the process of using her wrinkle remover, a heady smelling liquid that she patted on with bits of cotton and allowed to dry. After an allotted time, the top, thin layer of epidermis peeled off, like a snake shedding its skin.

I don't know whether or not it took off wrinkles, but Violet used it religiously until one day when Sam found it on the shelf in their walk-in closet. He held the unmarked bottle to the light and ran the tip of of his tongue over his lips at the sight of the bourbon-colored liquid. Then, pulling the cork, he raised the bottle to his lips and drained it dry. I can't imagine what it did to his stomach, but I do know that for over a week he was the sickest man I have ever seen, before or since.

Dad said it was the closest Sam had been to death's door since the time on the *Water Queen* showboat when he did the magic trick of changing water to wine and, carried away by the thunderous round of applause, drank the mixture of chemicals to prove it was real.

Fortunately, he recovered in time for our opening. The actors and crew were on board and the show was rehearsed. We opened on March 26 at Vesta and made our customary tour up and down the Monongahela.

Then we soared out into the Ohio headed for a change in our lifestyle that would be as exciting as going over a four-foot dam in a flatboat, something Dad always said everyone should experience at least once in his lifetime.

It was 1929.

THE RIGHT PLACE
AT THE
RIGHT TIME

When the Showboat Age began to wane, the giants were the first to go. Between 1916 and 1919, seven of the grand old floating theaters were lost. The *Hippodrome*, the *Dixie*, the *Illinois*, *Greater New York*, *French's New Sensation*, the *Cotton Blossom*, and the *Wonderland* were all destroyed by wind, ice, or fire. High operational costs and diminishing routes put some of the others out of business.

In the twenties, some showboats were still being built. But they were, like ours, smaller boats, and they roamed the hinterland, catering to the rural population, and playing every mile on every navigable stream.

Toward the end of the decade, paved roads and automobiles gave mobility to the heretofore captive audiences, and the showboat's monopoly on formal entertainment began to crumble.

Radio entered the scene, and though at first only two or three listeners shared a set of earphones attached to a "crystal set," it was only the beginning. Soon, the finest music, comedy and drama from the entertainment capitals of the country was blaring out of horn-shaped speakers, and kitchens were crowded with family members and friends laughing and crying together in the comfort of their own homes.

Nickelodeons and then proper movies spread to the villages, and productions like *Flesh and the Devil* with John Gilbert and Greta

Garbo and *Bella Donna* with Pola Negri contributed greatly to a
growing demand for a more sophisticated style of entertainment.

As the thirties loomed, even the smaller boats began dropping
by the wayside, and those that clung to life floundered and flopped
like fish caught in a shrinking pool of water. In the summer of 1929
Dad decided, as an experiment, to tie up for three nights at a city
landing. He chose Cincinnati. We docked at the foot of Lawrence
Street. Sam and the deckhand laid out a wide, sawdust-strewn path
to the top of the high bank. They could have made it much more
narrow for, on the first night, we had three people in the audience
and the second night, none. The third day Dad announced at breakfast
that everyone might as well go uptown that evening as there would be
no show on board and we would be moving on the next day.

Just at dusk, a huge yacht drifted slowly up against the outside
guard and a man wearing white pants, a blue blazer, an ascot, and a
captain's hat called to Dad, who was standing on our front deck.

"You there! Could you please catch this rope?" and he tossed
over the end of a line which Dad caught and secured to a ring in the
deck. The man continued, "We seem to be out of gas or something!"
Behind him, on the yacht, the members of his party roared with
laughter at what they seemed to think was a witty remark. "Any
objections to us laying over?" the man asked.

Dad not only had no objections, he even invited them to come on
board for a tour while our engineer took a look at their yacht's motor.
By now, Mother and I were on the deck, echoing Dad's invitation.

There were about fifteen in the party. Most of them were from
out of town and had never seen a showboat. They were as excited as
children at the prospect of seeing a show. When they found out that
we weren't performing that night they were so disappointed the owner of the yacht asked Dad if we would be willing to play *Ten Nights in
a Barroom* for twenty-five dollars. Dad said that for twenty-five dollars we would be willing to play *Strange Interlude*.

He alerted the actors, who were still on board, turned on the generator, and we did the show. To say it was a smash hit would be the understatement of the year. But it was also the most confusing night of the Bryants' entire career.

The group not only applauded the hero and shouted encouragement to the heroine, but when Joe Morgan delivered his denunciation of Demon Rum speech, they actually stood up in a body and cheered. They found the villain, with his handlebar mustache, to be the funniest thing they had ever seen, and they hissed and booed him unmercifully while wiping tears of laughter from their cheeks.

In the beginning, Dad was a bit confused by the unusual reaction, but he was nothing if not quick. By the end of the first act he realized what was happening and knew instinctively that, in the mine of entertainment, we had, somehow, struck the mother lode.

After the first act, he stepped out before the roll curtain and looked at the small, smiling group in the first two rows. Then he started to ad lib.

"Well, folks," he began, with a disarming smile, "I guess you didn't expect us to be good, and it's nice to know you haven't been disappointed." The audience roared.

"My dear old dad used to say, 'Blessed is he who expects nothing, for he shall never be deceived.'" (More laughter.) "You know, we're just a bunch of small-town river actors, but we love what we do, and that's worth a lot in this world today. To be a ham and not know it—that's pitiful! But to be a ham and *admit* it—*that's* something *beautiful!*"

It was the first presentation of the curtain speech that Dad was to develop to perfection and eventually deliver in cities from coast to coast with huzzahs and plaudits from audiences and critics alike.

He went on to invite the group to participate as much as they liked by hissing, booing, and cheering. He even suggested that, if the show got too bad, they could go home.

"We've got your money," he said, with charming sincerity. "If it gets to be worse than you bargained for, you can leave any time you want to. We'll understand." The audience screamed with laughter, and wild horses could not have pulled them from their seats.

After the show, Dad, Mother, and I went aboard the yacht and had night lunch with the guests. They were all in high spirits and complimented us profusely on the great "satire" we had put on.

One of the guests was named Moses Strauss. He introduced himself as the managing editor of the *Times Star* and nearly had apoplexy when he heard that we were leaving the next day. He told Dad he wasn't going to let him go until he had promised to stay at least one more night. Dad laughingly agreed, and we went back on board to wave our newfound friends off in their repaired yacht.

The next afternoon when Dad strolled uptown I trotted along at his side. I knew he was going to get the paper, and I wanted to see if Moses Strauss was who he said he was. He certainly was! The *Times Star* carried a beautiful story about the evening with a four-column headline welcoming the *Bryant's Showboat* as the most refreshing thing to hit Cincinnati in years.

That night, and every night for the next thirteen summers, we played to standing room only. Business built so fast that we had to install a telephone in the office, and we were selling seats to out-of-town parties six weeks in advance.

For some time the lifestyle in America had been changing too rapidly and people were beginning to feel the first labor pains in the birth of nostalgia. They came seeking a brief but comforting return to simpler times, and, when the show was over, like thousands of farmers before them, they lingered on the front deck, talking with the captain and members of the family, reluctant to sever the last delicate link with the past.

It was a perfect example of what can happen as a result of merely being in the right place at the right time.

CINCINNATI

We closed at Cincinnati that fall and went back to West Elizabeth for the winter. The next year we opened on the Monongahela and followed our usual route as far as Cincinnati, where we tied up for the summer. It was to be the second year of a run of thirteen years.

Requests for favorite melodramas started coming in and we changed shows every four weeks. Besides the old standards of *Ten Nights in a Barroom, Uncle Tom's Cabin,* and *East Lynne,* we did classics like *Tempest and Sunshine, Her Dead Sister's Secret, Thorns and Orange Blossoms,* and *Over the Hill to the Poorhouse.*

Dad never really burlesqued the shows. He would cut the scripts down and add clever bits of business and dialogue, but he always held to the basic script and insisted that the actors play their parts straight. He became so adept at it that the deliberate boners were usually accepted as the mistakes of bad direction and inadequate actors. Few people knew of the hours of painstaking rehearsal that went into perfecting those "errors."

The one spot on earth that inspired Dad to tyranny was the stage, and heaven help the actor who would ad lib, change a movement, or do anything in any way to give the impression that he thought what he was doing was funny.

The "mistakes" were strategically placed against a background of serious melodrama. When the roll curtain fell to the floor, catching the dead body in front of it, and in response to frantic "histing"

Showboat and *Valley Belle* at Cincinnati

from the corpse, was pulled up far enough for him to roll back up stage, it was hysterically funny, but only if the corpse didn't obviously think so.

Dad was a master at teaching the breakup, in which the actor appears to be suffering from a tickled funnybone and is trying not to laugh. It starts with a twinkle in the eye and a slight twitch at the side of the mouth, followed by a hiccup-like snort and then a series of shoulder shakes escalating to a point where the actor turns his back on the audience and seems to be laughing uncontrollably. The greatest exponent of the breakup in recent years was Johnny Carson.

The audiences were magnificent. Whereas the people in the little towns cried so much at the old melodramas that the plays became known as tearjerkers, our newfound clientele became such an integral part of the evening's entertainment that they seldom stopped laughing.

Later, when I became old enough to do grownup parts, in *No Mother to Guide Her*, I was being held prisoner in a room. But, there was a second key hidden on stage. Every night, during my frantic search for it, the audience would holler, en masse, "It's in the teapot!" They were never abusive or rude, and they never threw things on the stage or used coarse language. Their participation in the show was in a positive vein, and, in their own way, they were just as anti-villain, pro-leading-man, and determined to protect the purity of the ingenue as any audience that ever crossed our stage plank.

Sometimes, one of them would come up with a line worthy of a playwright. In *Agnes, the Switchman's Daughter*, in which I played the title role, the villain is a hypnotist who hypnotizes Agnes during the first act.

"Sleep, sleep," he drones. "Sleep, Agnes, you are now completely in my power. When you awaken, you will do my bidding as I command. Wake up, Agnes, *now!*"

I would seemingly come out of my trance and he would put me through a trial run.

"Agnes, come here." I would walk away.

"Agnes, leave me." I would walk toward him.

"Agnes, stand over there." I would sit down.

"Agnes, sit down!" I would stand up. He would look at the audience and say, "Gad zooks! I've hypnotized her backwards!"

One night we did the scene as usual.

"Agnes, come here." I walked away.

"Agnes, leave me." I walked toward him.

"Agnes, stand over there." I sat down.

"Agnes, sit down." I stood up.

Then a man in the audience yelled, "Just like my wife!"

During *Midnight in Chinatown*, at the end of the second act, a Chinese warlord, played by Doug Morris, chased me all around the stage, waving a wicked-looking sword over his head. I made my way through the box seats and out into the audience. I would run up one aisle and Doug would run up the opposite one.

Then, ignoring the screams and laughter of the people, I would excuse myself and go through the row of seats to the middle and stop while Doug did the same thing about four rows back. We would scoot back and forth a few feet, and all the while he would be swinging the sword over the people's heads and shouting threats at me. Finally, we would continue the chase. I would go back on stage, and when he followed me, I would deck him with an uppercut.

One night we had the entire membership of some fraternity in the theater. While Doug and I were in the rows, several of the boys got to their feet and with shouts of "You cur!" and "Never fear, ma'am, we'll save you!" they grabbed Doug around the waist, took his sword, pushed him into the aisle, and demanded that he leave.

Then, they escorted me back to the stage, bowed, and returned to their seats. Dad came on stage, complimented them on their daring rescue, and then asked for the sword back so we could finish the scene.

Around the middle of September, we would sell the house each night to sponsors, church groups, fraternal organizations, ladies' clubs, and such. They would pay a flat rate for all the tickets and then sell to their members. Mother's journal, in which she formerly listed the routes, was now filled with sponsors' names and their show dates.

October, 1934
 9—Sisters of the Blessed Sacrament
10—Hyde Park Masonic
11—Pi Omicron Sorority
12—Glendale Presbyterian Church
13—Union Gas and Electric
14—Lions Club
15—Ohio State Hairdressers
16—Daughters of the Nile
17—Knights of Columbus
18—Bellvue High School
19—Sigma Chi Fraternity
20—Norwood Democratic Club
21—Women's Mail Service

Every night five hundred people would come over the top of the riverbank and make their way down the rock-bordered path to see the same old melodramas and specialties we had been presenting at the small river landings.

Vic Faust was a sensation, as always, and they still whistled and waved to get one of Carl Adams's chalk talk drawings. When Clyde Shafer, our portly, mustached villain sang "Yip-Iaddy-I-Ay," the audience went wild. But when he rendered, under Dad's direction, his special arrangement of "A Man Was the Cause of It All," he stopped the show.

After warbling the verse, he went into the chorus:

> She's more to be pitied than censured.
> She's more to be helped than despised.
> She's only a lassy who ventured,
> On life's stormy path, ill advised.
> Do not scorn her with words fierce and bitter.
> Do not laugh at her shame and downfall.
> For a moment just stop (PAUSE) and consider.
> That a man . . .

Clyde would stop singing and point to an especially happy fellow in the first or second row. Revolving his finger in a circle, he would say, "Yes, you're one of them!" Then he would finish the song dramatically:

> Was the Cause . . . of . . . it . . . all!!!!!!

During the first five years in Cincinnati, besides my impersonations of George M. Cohan, Ted Lewis, and George S. Primrose and my novelty songs and dances, my toughie numbers were my biggest hits. Mother would dress me in a long-sleeved seater, a short, tight skirt with a slit on the side, a long pair of beads, and a hat with a flower sticking up in the front. I would sing either "When Francis Dances wid Me," "Every Night He Brings Me Wylets [Violets]," "I'm Gonna Dance wid da Guy What Brung Me," or my favorite, "Down by da Winiger Woiks [Vinegar Works]."

Verse
You've read about tough guys and places,
In books dat you keep on da shelf.
Well, I am so tough and at times I'm so rough,
I must be polite to meself.
Me pals is a couple of Bull Dogs.
Wid mustard I sweetens me tea.
Dere's only two guys in dis woild dat is tough
And both of dem babies is me!
Chorus
I live over da wydock, down by da winiger woiks.
It's easy to find me, da street's full of shacks.
I live in da one dat is right on da tracks.
Every night I go dancin', down at O'Riley's or Boik's.
Da kids smoke cigars when der seven weeks old,
Dey cry for Carbolic when dey gets a cold.
I live over da wydock, down by da winiger woiks.

Then, following in Dad's dance steps, I would do a waltz clog for the
first half of the second chorus and finish with,

We chain all da children to fences and logs.
We do it to keep 'em from bitin' da dogs.
I live over da wydock, down by da winiger woiks!

We were constantly in the news. The reporters loved Dad: he
was what they used to call "good copy." Tracy York of the *Chicago
Sun* would capture Dad's magic in his column under the heading
"Colorful? Billy Bryant shames the Rainbow!"

It was Quent Reynolds, ace correspondent, newspaperman, writer and
commentator on everything under the sun that ever came into his capacious
ken (in other words—everything) who made the most penetrating observa-
tion we recall having heard on color.

As Quent saw it, it wasn't so much a man's achievements that made
him interesting news as a certain quality of colorfulness, hard to define but
easy to spot. Quent pointed out that Babe Ruth had it—lots of it—and that
the late Lou Gehrig, for all his baseball playing and despite all the efforts of
a corps of high-pressure press agents, just didn't.

Anyway, all this preambling is merely to launch into a brief commentary on *the* man among men who is the living definition of color—one Billy Bryant.

Billy is handsome, neat, dignified and impressive. Billy is raffish, tough and gay. Billy is quiet. Billy is loud. Billy is a volatile, unpredictable, amazing man. Billy, friends, is a character.

Dad also knew how to get the most out of a story, and his ideas were current and sometimes deliberately controversial. When Margaret Mitchell's *Gone With the Wind* swept the nation, Dad dug out and doctored a long forgotten old melodrama about the Civil War and called it *Gone With the Breeze*.

When Bruna Castagna came to Cincinnati to do summer opera, Dad put on his version of *Carmen*, telling the press that his daughter Betty not only did a better Carmen than Miss Castagna, but she also did a tap dance between acts and played the front end of the bull. That got us a four-column story in every local paper plus a column and a half and a picture in *Time* magazine.

Dad was also lucky. Sometimes a story would just materialize out of the air, like the night a car came to the show. A young man and his date had nosed his car into a parking space right on top of the long and steep riverbank. A few minutes later, as the couple was about halfway down the path, his car came careening down the hill, passed them, and dove right into the river, under the guardrail. The next day the paper had a cartoon of them walking down the hill to the showboat and the car speeding past them. The girl was saying, "Pardon me, but isn't that your car?"

The Bryants and their showboat were as much a part of Cincinnati as the zoo, Coney Island, or the *Island Queen*. Later on, at the close of the final season, when, like Edna Ferber's Magnolia, I married the leading man, our wedding threatened to push the Second World War off the front pages of the *Cincinnati Enquirer*, the *Post*, and the *Times Star*.

A LADY AND A QUEEN

Our showboat was tied up at the foot of Lawrence Street, two blocks east of Broadway. Broadway was the site of the public landing where steamboats, packets and excursion boats docked. Two of our finest aquatic neighbors were moored there, the *Greene Line* and the *Island Queen*.

The *Queen* was a beautiful, sidewheel excursion boat that carried passengers to and from Coney Island, an amusement park situated ten miles up the river on the Ohio side. She had a capacity of four thousand people and a dance floor made of twenty thousand square feet of polished hardwood. At one end, a beautiful bandstand housed a large orchestra led by Clyde Trask.

A balcony, with little wicker rocking chairs, ran entirely around the dance floor. Constantly changing colored lights of red, green, yellow, and blue flooded the floor, and hundreds of couples danced to the strains of the music of the day, songs like "Pennies from Heaven," "Deep Purple," "When Did You Leave Heaven?" "I'll Never Smile Again," and "Bei Mir Bist Du Schon."

On the lower deck was a cafeteria. Up top, while the boat was loading and unloading at the landings, Homer Denny would play the calliope. The trip to Coney Island took an hour going upriver and forty-five minutes coming down. Along the way people on shore would wave, and generations of young men paddled canoes out to the boat to catch the swells and ride in the wake of her big sidewheels. A round-trip ticket, which included admittance to the park, cost thirty-five cents for an adult, twenty cents for a child.

The amusement park was one of the finest in the country. It began in 1880 as a picnic grove on the Kentucky side of the river. In 1886 it was sold. The new owners moved it to the other side of the river and named it "Ohio Grove . . . Coney Island of the West."

The park grew and grew, eventually boasting hundreds of rides, including two roller coasters called the Wildcat and the Shooting Star. Tickets for the rides were ten cents. Sometimes during the summer they would have Nickel Day, with everything going for five cents.

In 1924, under the management of Mr. George Shot, they added a gargantuan swimming pool. Then they built a dance pavilion, called the Moonlight Gardens, which became famous from coast to coast. For forty-two cents, patrons could enter and dance or just listen to the music of the great bands of the era such as Glenn Miller, Harry James, Benny Goodman, and the Dorseys.

From Tuesday through Friday the *Island Queen* made four round trips a day, starting at 11:00 A.M. from the Cincinnati landing, and ending with the last trip leaving Coney Island at 10:45 P.M. On Saturdays, Sundays, and holidays, she made two extra trips, leaving from the city at 10:15 and 11:30 P.M. from the park.

On her 9:15 trip from Coney Island, the *Queen* would pass our boats during a scene in the last act. We could hear her coming, and as she sailed past with the sound of her band and happy voices floating through our open windows, we always stood in tableau until she passed. Then, we would resume our dialogue to the delight of our audience.

Every Saturday or Sunday that I could get permission I would be on her final trip. As soon as the last customer left the showboat I would make a mad run along the riverbank, sometimes with my mother leading the way. We would leap over logs, sidestep rocks, and whoop and wave as we neared the boat. Usually, the captain or one of the deckhands would wave back and shout out encouragement. We would run up the gang plank, out of breath and exploding with laughter. To the sound of a whistle, complaining winches, and shouted orders, the paddle wheels would start to turn and the boat would pull away from the landing and head upstream.

Mother and I would go to the top deck where tiny benches were scattered about. The moonbeams furnished *very* indirect lighting, the breeze was cool and soft and the sound of music floated up from the bandstand below. It would be difficult to find a more romantic setting. We would make our way to the front of the boat, lean on the rail, and quietly enjoy the beauties of the river night.

The *Queen* started her season on Memorial Day and ended it on Labor Day. On that final trip each year she was always filled to capacity, and the mood was different. People laughed louder, danced harder, and kept moving all around the boat. The closer they came to the end of the trip, the more tense they seemed to be.

Finally, she passed the landing to make her big sweeping turn a few yards down stream. The band stopped and the passengers crowded together on the front deck, waiting to disembark. Homer Denny would start playing the calliope. He would play a medley of what he called "departure tunes." "Meet Me Tonight in Dreamland," "My Wild Irish Rose," and "Annie Laurie." Then for the one and only time during the season, he would play "Jerusalem, the Holy City."

No matter how many people were on board, they all stood quietly and listened, probably thinking of the fine times they had had on board the beautiful boat all summer and perhaps planning ahead for another season with the *Queen*.

Next to the *Island Queen* landing floated the wharf boats owned by the Greene Line. Depending on their schedules, at least one of their five steamboats was usually moored there. On board would probably be one of the dearest, sweetest, most lovable pilots ever to blow a whistle or ring a bell—Captain Mary Becker Greene.

On one summer day in 1939 I went to visit her. At the time I was writing and selling articles to various river publications, and she had agreed to be interviewed. We had been friends for several years, and I knew a leading question or two would be all that was needed to reap a wonderful story. I don't know why I never submitted the article, but I am very glad that I kept it in my files. She was so much a part of the river.

Lady Captain

"Ma Greene," as she is affectionately called by those who know and love her, sat in a willow rocker on the upper deck of the steamer *Gordon C. Greene*. In her lap was an apron made of four gay, voile handkerchiefs, and as she talked, she sewed.

"I'm making them for the church," she explained. "I've already turned in seventy-eight dollars, and I still have a lot more aprons. Our passengers like them for souvenirs."

Seventy-two years ago, this genteel lady began life as little Mary Becker at Hills, Ohio near Marietta on the Little Muskingum River. She grew to maturity in the shadows of a cracker box and a mail sack in her father's combination post office and general store. Her days were filled with lessons from her mother in cooking and sewing, helping her father, and attending the village school.

It was there that she first met Gordon Greene. Their childhood friendship developed, as the years passed, into a true and beautiful devotion. And in 1890, Captain Greene claimed her as his bride. The following day they went by train to their new home, Gordon's first steamboat, the *H.K. Bedford*. "The pilot house was really my home," she explains today. "I was in there with Gordon most of the time, and I couldn't help but learn the river. In three years I received my license, and a year later, my captain's papers. My license covers the river from Parkersburg to Pittsburgh, first class, any tonnage.

"Six years after we were married, we launched the *Argand*, a little one-boiler boat. Gordon was taking the *Bedford* to Cincinnati so I took command of the *Argand*." She ran from Pittsburgh to Charleston, West Virginia.

"I never went on the roof in the daytime," she said, with a

delightful smile. "People looked at me like I had horns. They couldn't imagine me being a lady captain.

"I hired the crew myself and stood watch till one. The first week we made six dollars and sixteen cents. That's nothing for a steamboat. But after that we made between fifty and two hundred and fifty dollars a week.

"The rudders on that boat were awful heavy so I hired a boy by the name of Jesse Hughes to cub for me.

"We stopped at every dog path those days. One day we saw a woman waving to us from a path on the bank. I was in the pilot house with Jesse. We nosed 'er in and landed. Then I called down to her and said, 'What do you want to ship?'

"By that time we had the plank out. She answered, 'Oh, I didn't want anything, I was waving to a girl I knew.' The girl ran down the plank and they kissed each other. I yelled, 'Is that all?' They said, 'Yes.' My passenger came back on and we went on down the river. We'd just stopped to let those two girls kiss!

"Jesse Hughes has been with us ever since those first boatin' days. He's vice president of the line now, and he's just like my adopted son.

"I've had three boys of my own, you know. Wilkens, the oldest, was born in 1898. He died when he was nine. In 1901 Chris arrived and the same year we got the first *Evergreen*. They sort of grew up together, Chris and the *Evergreen*, and in 1913 we renamed her the *Chris Greene*.

"In 1904 I took command of the *Greenland*. I had a five-room cabin and bath on 'er, and I kept a woman to take care of Wilkins and Chris. Right after we brought her out, we had to tie up at Point Pleasant, West Virginia, on account of an ice run out in the Ohio. It was there that Tom was born. We'd had a doctor and other arrangements made at my mother's home in Marietta, but Tom got there six weeks early.

"The *Greenland* was the only side-wheeler we ever owned. She sank, here at Cincinnati." It's obviously hard for Mary Greene to distinguish between her boys and her boats, for they are both held in equal pride.

In 1927, Captain Gordon C. Greene died at his home in Hyde Park. The year before, Tom had returned from the University at Columbus in order to learn navigation under the able tutorage of his father.

Ma Greene, her eyes pregnant with memories, stared out across the water.

"I know Gordon would be proud of his boys if he were here today," she said. "They're fine pilots and fine men.

"We have five boats in the line now. There's the *Tom Greene*, the *Chris Greene*, the *Evergreen*, the *Cary Bird*, and this one, the *Gordon C. Greene*. This is the only passenger boat on the river today. She carries two hundred and twenty-five people and has three rudders, weighin' over a ton each. She has accommodations just as good as most hotels.

"We go out tomorrow, you know, and I'm glad. I love the trips and the people. They seem to have an awfully good time, and they write me such nice letters when they leave. We have entertainment going on all the time, and I never get tired, even now. I still dance every night until the music stops at eleven o'clock.

"There goes the *Cary Bird*," she said, interrupting herself. "Watch 'er as she turns around. She's white and beautiful, and she sits on the water like a swan. You know, I've always lived where I could see the river and I've been boatin' for fifty years, and yet I never fail to get all tingly inside whenever I see how gracefully one of our boats pulls out from shore.

"This is my home," she continued. "I love it here. The boys can't understand why I don't stay up at the house more, but the river is so beautiful.

"Sometimes I tell Tom I'm goin' home with Chris and then I tell Chris I'm goin' home with Tom. It's the only way I can get a peaceful night's rest without them worryin' about me.

"I wish you'd kinda take notice of the wharf boats as you leave.

We bought five new ones just this summer. The boys are mighty proud of the Greene Line, and they take mighty good care of it.

"I may be over to see you tonight, but then I've worked pretty hard today. Not that I'm tired, mind you. But there's always a lot to do on the night before we leave.

"Come and see me again when we get back from New Orleans. I love to have company . . . especially when they like to talk about the river."

The last time I saw Ma Greene was in 1942 at my wedding during our last season in Cincinnati. She passed away in 1949 and now holds an honored place in the National Rivers Hall of Fame in the Woodward Riverboat Museum at Dubuque, Iowa.

The *Island Queen* was destroyed by an explosion and fire at Pittsburgh, Pennsylvania, in 1947.

LURE OF CITY LIGHTS

At the end of the 1930 season, we tied up to winter at West Elizabeth for what was to be the last time. In the spring of '31, Dad received a letter from a Pittsburgh friend by the name of George Sharp. Sharp said he was in the throes of producing *Ten Nights in a Barroom* for a one-week engagement at the Shubert Pitt Theater in Pittsburgh and was having difficulty casting a little girl for the part of Mary Morgan and the comic, Sample Swichel. He knew Dad had done Swichel on the showboat for years and I already had two seasons of Mary Morgan to my credit. Sharp asked Dad if we would be willing to do the roles. Dad agreed, and we began to commute from West Elizabeth to Pittsburgh by train.

Ten Nights in a Barroom, one of the two most popular plays in the history of the American theater, was written as a temperance play, but Dad said it probably drove more people to drink than it saved. Much of the story revolves around Joe Morgan, his long suffering wife, Fanny, and their little daughter, Mary. Joe, a slave to the Demon Rum, makes daily trips to the local tavern, and every night his little girl comes to find him and tearfully lead him home while singing,

> Father, dear Father, come home with me now.
> The clock in the steeple strikes one.
> You promised, dear Father, that you would come home

Betty portrayed Mary Morgan in *Ten Nights in a Barroom* at Studebaker
Theater in Chicago: "Father, dear Father, come home with me now."
Betty's grandfather Sam is at far left.

As soon as your day's work was done.
Come home, come home,
Dear Father, dear Father, come home!"

They pause as Morgan turns to the proprietor and says, "Simon
Slade, you have robbed me of my last farthing, but this little trea-
sure still remains. Come child, I'll go, I'll go."

A few scenes later, Morgan has returned to the tavern, and Simon Slade is trying to make him leave.

SLADE: Off with you, Joe Morgan. I won't put up with your insolence any
longer. If you can't be decent, and *stay* decent, don't intrude yourself here.
MORGAN: You talk of decency, a rum seller's decency! Bah! You were a
decent man once and a good miller into the bargain but that time is long

"Father, dear Father, they have killed me!"

gone. Decency died out when you exchanged the pick and facing hammer
for the glass and tumbler. Decency? Bah! How like a fool you talk. As if it
were any more decent to *sell* rum that it is to drink it!
SLADE: I've had enough of your insults. Now, leave my house and never
come back here again!
MORGAN: I won't!
SLADE: Then, curse you, take that!

He throws a glass at Morgan's head. It misses him and flies off stage
into the wings where Mary is waiting. She rushes in, with her fore-
head dripping carmine blood, screaming, "Father, dear Father, they
have killed me!" and falls into the arms of Willie Hammond.

The next scene is in the Morgan home. Mary is in bed, asleep.
Her head is swathed in a bloody bandage. Joe is sitting by the bed.
His wife, Fanny, leaves to get the doctor. Mary wakes up and speaks.

"Oh, Father, I had the most wonderful dream." Then, under

soft, blue lights, to the tune of "Hearts and Flowers," she describes the dream.

I thought it was night and I was still sick. You promised not to go out again until I got well, but you did go out and I thought you went to Mr. Slade's Tavern. All at once, I felt so strong and I got up and started after you.

At last I came to Mr. Slade's Tavern and there you were, Father, standing in the doorway but you were dressed so nice. You had on a new hat and a new coat and I said, "Oh, Father, is this you?" And you took me up in your arms and kissed me and said, "Yes, Mary."

It was all so strange for there wasn't any barroom there any longer, but a store full of goods and over the door I read your name, Father. I was so happy. But then I woke and I started to cry for it was only a dream.

Overcome with the sad beauty of it all, her father promises to reform, and Mary dies. In his grief, Joe Morgan suffers an attack of delirium tremens. He begins to scream and falls to the floor, writhing and moaning. He clutches the bedclothes, pulls himself to his feet, runs in circles, spins blindly and kicks at invisible snakes and spiders, all the while pleading, "Take them off! Take them off! Fanny! Fanny! Take them off! Oh wife, my brain is on fire. Hideous visions are before my eyes. Look! Look! See! What's that? There! there, in the corner?"

Fanny replies, "There's nothing there, Joe."

He continues to rave. "There is, I tell you. I can see as well as you! Look! A huge snake is twining itself around my arms. Take him off! Take him off! Quick! Quick!

"So, you've come for me? Well, I'm ready. How bright they look, their eyes are glaring at me, and they're leaping and dancing and shouting with joy to think that the drunkard's hour has come!

"Keep them off! Keep them off! Oh, *Horror! Horror! Horror!*" The curtain descends as he falls across the bed, exhausted.

Ten years pass. In the last act Joe, his wife and their friends are standing in the Morgan's parlor drinking tea and talking of the many tragedies of the past decade, all brought on by alcohol. As they speak of Mary, she appears behind them in the transformation scene.

When we first arrived in Pittsburgh, Dad introduced me to Mr. Sharp. He was very kind and polite, but he told me that I was going to have a double who would do the transformation scene, as he was sending Mary to heaven straight from the death bed instead of waiting till the last act.

Though I never mentioned it, I didn't think it was a very good idea. The transformation had always been my favorite scene. But I shouldn't have given it a single thought, for that departure from the original play was nothing compared to what was yet to come.

When I died after my dream speech and Joe Morgan began to see things, we *all* began to see things! Spinning, color-wheel spots turned the room to red, blue, green, and yellow, and little rubber spiders fell to the floor and the bed. Three long battens were lowered behind the masking. Each batten had tied to it, by black threads of different lengths, dozens of brightly painted, wooden, wriggling reptiles.

Joe Morgan screamed for his wife, and mechanical mice raced across the floor. Then, with a green travel spot following him, he backed into a corner screeching and a six-man-power Chinese dragon undulated out of the closet spewing red fire from its grinning, papier-mache mouth. Corpse or no corpse, I wouldn't have closed my eyes for an Academy Award!

I guess nobody noticed because Florence Fisher Parry of the *Pittsburgh Press* gave the play a fine review. She complimented each member of the cast individually and said in closing, "And—and most important of all—a regular little Eva by the name of Betty Bryant playing the only absolutely straight part in the piece, and playing it to the hilt, God Bless her earnest little heart."

At the end of the week, back on the showboat, we went immediately into rehearsal for our season opening. An added bonus from our appearance at the Pitt Theater was our meeting with Clyde

Shafer, a rather portly and extremely dignified actor who played a small part in the play.

Clyde started his career in the theater at the age of six in *Vesper Bells*. Later, he toured the small circuits in vaudeville with a singing act. In the First World War he spent eighteen months overseas. Upon returning home, he went to work in stock in Pittsburgh. When *Ten Nights in a Barroom* closed, he applied for a job on the showboat, and Dad hired him on the spot. He was a fabulous villain and stayed with us until he passed away in 1934.

At the end of that summer of 1931, in Cincinnati, Dad received a phone call from a Chicago theatrical producer by the name of George Wintz. Mr. Wintz had read a story in the *Chicago Tribune* by the drama critic, Charles Collins about our success in Cincinnati, in which Collins asked, "Why can't we have a showboat in Chicago?" George Wintz wanted us to bring the showboat up the Chicago River. But when Dad explained how impractical, if not impossible, that would be, Mr. Wintz hung up. About an hour later he called back and said that everything had been arranged for us to bring the show to the Studebaker Theater.

The family discussed the idea at length and finally agreed to give it a try. At the end of the season Dad kept the cast together, brushed up *Ten Nights in a Barroom* and headed for Chicago.

We opened at the Studebaker on November 22, 1931. Ticket prices were twenty-five cents, fifty cents, seventy-five cents, and a dollar.

On opening night, the critics were there from all of the newspapers, and, after seeing the show and listening to Dad's curtain speech, they went back to their typewriters in a state of near shock. Unanimously, they agreed that when Dad stepped out after the first act and told the audience he knew the show was terrible but that the actors were all just showboat hams who were scared to death but doing the very best they could, he stopped them cold.

If they didn't like the show, all Dad left for them to do was agree with him. In his criticism of the performance, he was not embarrassed, glib, or unhappy. "If you didn't like the first act, you won't like the second one, because it gets worse." The crowd roared. He went on to explain that if it got too bad for them, they could leave, and it wouldn't hurt anyone's feelings. The audience and the critics ate it up. Then he broke every rule in the book by inviting them to come up on the stage during the intermission and have a glass of near beer with the members of the cast and enjoy the free lunch at the bar provided by Lindy's Famous Restaurant of Famous Foods.

The next morning, when the reviews came out, among other things, Fritz Blocki wrote, "Genuwine backwoods philosopher!" Lloyd Lewis said, "Nothing better in the Loop!" And Charley Collins of the *Tribune* wrote, "What a play! What a Troupe! A night worth remembering!"

We were at the Studebaker for six weeks. During that time, we were interviewed, photographed, and wined and dined like stars. One night we attended a party at the College Inn as Ben Bernie's guests, and, just before Christmas, we had dinner on the 185-foot diesel yacht *Mizpah* with its river commander E.F. McDonald, Jr. It was a heady atmosphere for a nine-year-old.

At the end of the six weeks we had to leave the Studebaker to allow the previously booked *Elizabeth the Queen* to open. We moved to the Cort Theater for two weeks and changed the play to *East Lynne*.

During our stay there, George Wintz was contacted by John Golden from New York. He had heard of our success, had the show checked out, and on the strength of the report, wanted us to play the John Golden Theater in New York. After we closed in Chicago we went to New York and opened with *Ten Nights in a Barroom* on January 20, 1932, for a ten-week run.

Backstage on opening night Dad made no bones about the fact that he was nervous. The first-nighters had turned out in force, and the house was filled to capacity with some of the biggest names in show business, politics, journalism, and sports.

Published for CORT THEATER

GEORGE E. WINTZ
presents

Billy Bryant's Show Boat Troupe
in that
BRILLIANT DRAMA OF TEARS AND
THRILLS THAT TEST A WOMAN'S SOUL

EAST LYNNE

Adapted from the Famous Novel
by
MRS. HENRY WOOD

Presented for the First Time in America
Tripler's Hall, New York City, March 23, 1863

Note: It is interesting to know that Mr. Sam Bryant, who enacts the role of
the policeman was born in the town of East Lynne, England,
where this play was written.

CAST OF PLAY
PROGRAMME

CHARACTERS	ARTISTS
Sir Francis Levison	CLYDE SHAFFER
Archibald Carlyle	MACK FRANKS
Lord Mount Severn	CARL CARLTON
Mr. Dill	BILLY BRYANT
Police Officer	SAM BRYANT
Richard Hare	FRANK ANTON
Barbara Hare	
Miss Cornelia Carlyle	JANE KERMIT
Joyce	FLORENCE REYNOLDS
Susanne	JOAN MEYER
Lady Isabel ⎱ Dual Role	
Madam Vine ⎰	JOSEPHINE BRYANT
Little Willie	BETTY BRYANT

SYNOPSIS OF SCENES
Act I

Parlor in Archibald Carlyle's House at East Lynne. Arrival in East
Lynne.

GRAND INTERMISSION

All Patrons are invited during this intermission to come back on the
stage, visit with our Artists, share in MRS. KLIEN'S Potato Chips and
step up to the bar and quench their thirst with a couple or three steins of
that delicious PRIMA'S SPECIAL BEER with our compliments. You will
find entrance to the stage on the extreme left aisle of the theatre.

Act 2

Scene 1—Lady Isabel's apartment in the Tenement District of London.
Scene 2—The Public Square at East Lynne.
Scene 3—Archibald Carlyle's home. The arrival of Madame Vine.

Act 3

Scene 1—The Carlyle Home. Death of Little Willie.
Scene 2—The Public Square at East Lynne.
Scene 3—Carlyle's Home. Death of Lady Isabel. "Farewell—Until
Eternity."

Note: During the action of the play the following artists will render
versatile musical interpretations:

CLYDE SHAFFER	Songs of the Gay Nineties
JANE KERMIT	By the Sea
PAUL ROBINSON	Harmonica
BETTY BRYANT	Impersonation of Geo. M. Cohan at the age of 7
VIC FAUST	Fiddle and Swiss Bells

PRIMA SPECIAL BEER served back stage is with compliments of
Mr. Arnold of the Prima Brewing Company, makers of the best and purest
beer ever brewed.

He needn't have worried. If Dad's curtain speech was a hit in Chicago, it was a riot in New York. Again he disarmed the critics, and again he invited the audience to come onstage during the intermission for a glass of beer and free lunch, this time furnished by Noll Biscuit Co., Uneeda Bakers, Phoenix Kraft Cheese, and Tammers Malt Brew. Odd McIntyre got up from his seat and led the parade. It was a wonderful sight to see those distinguished ladies and gentlemen in their formal attire climbing up on stage and bellying up to the bar alongside of Joe Morgan, his wife, Fanny, and the rest of the cast. People like Fannie Hurst, Rube Goldberg, Robert Garland, John Mason Brown, Percy Hammond, Alfred E. Smith, Gene Tunney, and Charles Dana Gibson, all exchanging stories with the family and the actors, and everyone roaring with laughter.

The next day, the critics were even more enthusiastic than in Chicago, and they all praised Dad's curtain speech, comparing him favorably with Fred Allen, Nikita Balieff, Al Jolson, and Will Rogers.

We were at the John Golden Theater for ten weeks and could have stayed longer, but the worms in Central Park had started to surface and we knew their cousins on the Ohio River banks were doing the same. It was definitely time to go home.

It was during this time that Dad began publicly talking and writing about his greatest disappointment in life: the fact that no one would ever take him seriously as an actor. Perhaps (although I doubt it) in his early years, Dad may have had a longing to do dramatic parts. But once he recognized the value of the contrast of this unfulfilled dream to his image as a carefree buffoon, he used it to hone his comedic genius to a razor's sharpness. He played the indignant clown to the hilt and did it so well that even some of the greatest writers of the day were completely taken in.

Dad's scrapbook is filled with notices, all raving about his ability as a monologist. But, almost to a man, the critics laughingly agreed with him when he said, "The show is lousy, and I am just a showboat ham actor."

One of the rare ones who saw through the facade was Percy Hammond of the *New York Herald* who wrote:

It seems to be the impression hereabouts that Mr. Billy Bryant's Showboat actors are a troupe of country jakes, unused to the ways of a great city. That their interpretation of "Ten Nights in a Bar Room" is the innocent effort of rustic "hams" who realize their incompetence and accept the jeers of their audiences with becoming humility. In that opinion the local drama lovers err.

Mr. Bryant and his companions are sophisticated travesty artists, more at home in a Broadway playhouse than they would be in a lowly town hall on the lark and linnet circuit. In Cincinnati, where their vessel is anchored, they are recognized as expert spoofers, as they are in Chicago, another haven. Fresh from the polishing influences of these urban capitals, they burlesque poor old "Ten Nights in a Bar Room" with all the glee of a city slicker baiting a hayseed.

In Mr. Bryant himself New York has found a refreshing clown. It is he, who, after the first act, addressed the audience in a confession of his company's inabilities, admitting that they are "a bunch of old-fashioned, tall-grass hams." With a guile learned through selling corn-salve and electric belts from the tail gate of a medicine cart, Mr. Bryant hypnotizes his hearers into the belief that he is in earnest. "If you think we're rotten in this," he says, "you ought to see us do Hamlet."

All of this he does without much exposing the tongue in his cheek, and he seems to be just a nice, simple pilgrim from the Sears-Roebuck districts, trying to make himself at home. Mr. Golden finds in his monologue a resemblance to, but not an imitation of Mr. Will Rogers. It is said that other managers also have discerned a likeness and that Mr. Bryant is being solicited to remain in New York.

For eleven years, Dad spent his winters in the cities with his family and friends including Odd McIntyre, John Golden, George M. Cohan, Flo Zigfield, and Mike Todd and his summers on his beloved river where he was lionized as the owner of what had become one of Cincinnati's better known institutions.

A captain's paradise indeed!

OLIO

Nineteen thirty-one was also the year that Dad decided to change our winter quarters from West Elizabeth, Pennsylvania, to Henderson, West Virginia, a little village directly across the Kanawha River from Point Pleasant. Both towns lay at the top of a high stretch of riverbank that afforded boats excellent shelter during the winter storms.

This also altered our route. We no longer played the Monongahela or the upper Ohio. Instead, we went up the Kanawha to Charleston, West Virginia, in the spring. The people there, as in the other cities we now played were delighted with our brand of escapism, and they swarmed to the landing.

We would stay from four to six weeks, changing shows every week. At the end of that time, we would head back to the Ohio River. Breaking our jumps at towns like Gallipolis and Ironton, Ohio, we played a week or two at Huntington, West Virginia, and another at Portsmouth, Ohio. Then we tied up at Cincinnati for the summer.

With less traveling to do, we did not need a steamboat as large as the *Valley Belle*. During the thirteen summers we spent in Cincinnati, Dad replaced it first with the *Clairmont* and then with the *New Lotus*.

Attendance never dropped off. Some people would come back

again and again to see the same show over and over, exactly like the farmers who used to follow us from town to town. And when out-of-town friends came to visit them, the first place they would bring them was to the showboat.

Being in one town for such a long time was, at first, strange for me. I missed the old lifestyle, the shady willows, dusty lanes, and the waters that were clean and clear. I thought often of my giant sandpiles, favorite fishing holes, and private skating rinks on the idle excursion boats.

But, for the first time in my life, I did have the same children to play with every day. A wonderful family by the name of Nicholas owned a grocery store about a block back from the top of the riverbank. They practically adopted Mother and me, and I spent many hours in their home adjoining the store.

Other afternoons there were theaters to attend, baseball games to see, and excursions to Coney Island and the zoo to be enjoyed. Even then the Cincinnati Zoo was outstanding, with wooded picnic areas, lovely walks, a large, roofed pavilion, and a good selection of well cared for animals.

Each year, two weeks before Labor Day, the zoo would hold a food show. Large companies and small businesses would set up booths along the graveled paths, and each of them gave away samples of their products. Little paper cups of soup, sauces, slaws, and salad; diced cheese, ham, salami, chicken, beef, and tongue; platters of crackers covered with various kinds of spreads and little bottles of juices and soft drinks; dozens of booths and hundreds of free items brought people out in droves.

In 1936, we were engaged to appear, for two weeks, at the pavilion during the food show. The first week we played *Ten Nights in a Barroom* and the second week, *Heart of the Blue Ridge*. We did one performance a night and had standing room only. It was such a success they had us back the following year when we played *Jesse James* and *Nellie, the Beautiful Cloak Model*.

Many stars came through Cincinnati in those days. Some were touring with road show companies of New York shows, others were doing lectures or concerts. Some of them were appearing at Beverly Hills or the Gibson Hotel while still others were playing in vaudeville at the Keith Albee Theater. Many of them came to visit the boats, and, when their schedules permitted, they stayed to see the show.

Lily Pons sat in the balcony for one performance, laughing and applauding throughout the entire evening. She ate popcorn, bought prize candy, and delighted the audience by joining in the community singing.

Fifi D'Orsey obliged the newspaper photographers by appearing in a bathing suit on top of the showboat, pretending to be diving into the river, and Harry Langdon posed at the wheel in the pilot house.

Tallulah Bankhead, who was touring in *The Little Foxes*, not only saw the show but came early and spent several hours on the boat going over it like a conscientious building inspector. Finally, she signed her autograph on the wall in my room.

The Keith Albee Theater booked a different show each week, and I never missed a one. All the acts were splendid, and in practically every production a star would headline the bill.

I will never forget the week I saw John Boles, a very handsome musical comedy star from New York who was also gaining stature in Hollywood. Actually, I never really saw him perform. He was closing the bill, following an elephant act. As the huge pachyderms were circling the stage, one of them fell, with a tremendous crash, through the floor. She was sitting up with her front legs still on the stage and her trunk waving in the air. A stagehand quickly closed the traveler (a heavy curtain which is split in the middle). Over the loud speaker the stage manager introduced Mr. John Boles.

The orchestra played his introduction as he made his entrance from the side, in front of the curtain. He walked to the center of the stage where the mike stood. He smiled and opened his mouth to sing, but all the audience heard was an unhappy elephant's roar.

"URRRRRRRURRRRRRRURRRRRRRURRRRRRRUH!"

The music stopped. Mr. Boles smiled, and the crowd laughed and applauded. Again the orchestra played the introduction, again Mr. Boles opened his mouth, and again the elephant roared.

"URRRRRRRURRRRRRRURRRRRRRURRRRRRRUH!" Her timing was uncanny.

Once more the orchestra played the introduction, and once more Mr. Boles opened his mouth to sing but when the elephant roared, he merely pressed his nose against his right shoulder and waving his right arm in the air like an elephant's trunk, he lumbered off stage to

"URRRRRRRURRRRRRRURRRRRRRURRRRRRRUH!"

The manager announced that there would be a delay before the next show, and anyone wishing to leave could pick up a free pass for some future date. The orchestra played a circus march and the crowd filed out. I didn't even stop at the box office. I really felt I had had my money's worth.

The theater called in all sorts of experts, and in the end they had to rip out an elephant-sized piece of the outside wall, enlarge the hole in the stage, and lead the unhurt but very indignant animal through the band room and out to the street.

As the years passed, my parts in the plays became longer and more important, from Little Willie in *East Lynne* to Elsie in *The Fatal Wedding* and the little crippled girl in *The Miracle Woman*. In *Uncle Tom's Cabin*, like Topsy, "I just grew." I started as Eliza's baby, being carried across the ice, then I became Little Eva, grew into the part of Topsy, and finally graduated to the role of Eliza, carrying a baby doll across the ice.

Mary Morgan was the only character who absolutely refused to let me outgrow her. I played her in nearly every town on the Monongahela, Ohio, Kanawha, Kentucky, Big Sandy, upper Mississippi, and Illinois rivers. I played her in Pittsburgh, Chicago, and New York. I played her at the ages of seven, eight, nine, ten, eleven, twelve, thirteen, and fourteen. At that point, I was almost as tall as Joe Morgan, and I pleaded with Dad to do something about it. As usual, he came up with a wonderful idea.

Each time we headed for another town like Charleston, Huntington, or Portsmouth, he would call some official there and tell them that we needed a little girl to play Mary Morgan in *Ten Nights in a Barroom* for one of the weeks we were to be in their town. If they knew of anyone with a talented child who would be interested, please let us know. Within an hour we would receive a message from anyone from the school superintendent to the mayor saying that he had a daughter who would be happy to do the part. Dad would cut the dream speech to the bone and mail the part ahead.

When we arrived in the town, the mother with her child in tow would be waiting at the landing. After one short rehearsal of her scenes, Dad would give her the costume and tell her when we were doing the show.

It was a great success. We received fantastic publicity, and everyone came to see the local star. The child was happy, her parents were happy, Dad was happy, and I was delirious with joy. Everything went well until we went to Portsmouth.

All of the arrangements had been made. The child and her mother were at the landing in the morning. She rehearsed, accepted her costume, and went home.

That night, fifteen minutes before curtain, the little girl's mother came running up the stage plank carrying Mary Morgan's dress, shawl, and wig. thrusting them into Dad's hands, she mumbled something about her daughter having the chicken pox and fled.

Once more, I found myself loping across the stage like a wounded buffalo, screaming, "Father, dear Father! They have killed me!" and wishing they had.

In 1933, the radio station WLW signed us to do a weekly show on Thursday nights. It was to be broadcast live, from the showboat stage, at ten o'clock, following our regular performance. The audience was invited to stay and participate.

The program started without introduction, following an impressive number of dead air seconds. Then blew the haunting deep-throated whistle of the *Valley Belle*. After a pause, the announcer said "Here comes the showboat!"

The first night we came on the air, a four-year-old boy sat on the living room floor in front of the radio in his home at Henderson, West Virginia. The little village was almost totally made up of river families, and every man, woman and child could recognize any boat on the river by the sound of its whistle.

When this little fellow, sitting on the floor in front of the radio, heard the whistle blow, he jumped up, ran to his mother in the kitchen, and shouted, "Mama! Mama! Here comes 'at ton-of-a-bitch of a *Balley Belle*!"

RAININ' AND RISIN'

During the time we wintered in Henderson, West Virginia, we would often row across the Kanawha River or walk across the Point Pleasant-Henderson bridge to get our mail at the Point Pleasant Post Office. On Saturday nights we would go over to see the movies. For a few weeks each year I went to junior high and high school there, and every spring I would walk through the plowed fields looking for and sometimes finding arrowheads.

I have always loved Point Pleasant. It's a lovely, friendly, old river town that sits right on the point of land where the Big Kanawha River runs into the Ohio. The Indians called it "Tui-Endie-Wei" ("where the waters mingle"). It was a meeting place for many Indian tribes, and, although it took over a hundred years for the government to acknowledge it, it was the site of the first battle of the American Revolution, fought on October 10, 1774, between eleven hundred Virginia backwoodsmen under the command of Brigadier General Andrew Lewis and an equal number of Indian braves led by Cornstalk, chief of the Shawnees. It ended in a nervous treaty, with little satisfaction to either side.

Three years later, Cornstalk, who had tried desperately to maintain the peace, was murdered along with his son. According to a witness, he lay for several hours, mortally wounded. Legend has it that, on his deathbed, he called upon the Great Spirit to bear witness to the infamy of the White Eyes and, with his last gasping breath, placed a curse upon the scene of their treachery.

Whether or not the misfortunes the town endured in succeeding years were in any way connected to the Curse of Cornstalk, the possibility did lend a titillating aura of mystery to the town's pretty little park, where an eighty-four-foot granite shaft honors those who fought in the battle of Point Pleasant. Near the courthouse, in a simple grave outlined by a chain attached to four wooden posts, Cornstalk rests. One can hardly help but wonder.

Every spring the town would be threatened by floods. Sometimes the river would rise, teasingly, just to the top of the bank. Other times it would overflow into riverside homes. In January, they might see a change in the river's stage, but usually it was nothing too dramatic, until 1937.

We woke one morning during the second week in January to the sound of rain beating a frantic tattoo on the tar paper roof. We dressed hurriedly in a silence imposed by an unnatural feeling of urgency. Mother went to make coffee. The rest of us gathered on the shoreside guard and leaned on the rail.

It was plain to see that the river was on the rise. Dad put a marker at the water's edge, and then he and Leo tied the longest line we had around the base of a tall cottonwood tree. After a trip to the galley for a cup of coffee, Dad came back and checked the marker. In less than thirty minutes, the river had risen two inches.

All morning we watched the rate of the water's climb. By noon, both the marker and the line were totally submerged. Dad put a second line out higher on the tree, and, as the water rose, carrying the boat with it, he snaked the rope higher up the trunk. At the same time, we fed more line to the rope tied under the water. This way, no matter how high the river and the boat went, even if we eventually ran out of tree, the line at the base would act as a makeshift anchor.

The rain continued to pour down all that day and all through the night, and the water rose faster and faster. Occasionally, some-

Billy and Betty at the post office in Point Pleasant, West Virginia,
during the flood of 1937

one would row by in a skiff, and, in response to the call of, "What's
she doin' up river?" came the dreaded reply, "Rainin' and risin'!"

The next day we watched, with morbid fascination, as the river
flowed over the top of the banks. All day long the water spread farther
and farther, creeping silently over the fields, across the roads, through
the village of Henderson, and into the buildings.

By the third day, our line was tied to the middle of the cottonwood tree, and the water had spread in every direction as far as the
eye could see. Along the little road that led into Henderson, chickens roosted on telephone wires, their tails dipping into the water as
they wobbled on their precarious perch.

We did not know it at the time, but on January 9, the river at
Cairo had broken its banks and was backing up all the way to Pittsburgh. We were about to float through the worst flood in the history of the Ohio Valley.

Between the ninth and the twenty-sixth of January, when the crest of the flood would be reached, with the river at a 79.99-foot flood stage in Cincinnati, sixty-five thousand people became homeless in Hamilton County, Ohio, and in Northern Kentucky. Thirty thousand people in greater Cincinnati alone. And on January 24, "Black Sunday," at 10:30 A.M., a trolley wire broke and fell into the water in the industrial district, igniting the oil floating on the surface and creating a raging inferno. A three and a half mile front of fire completely enveloped the eight-story Crosley Building and three large factories. Bursting barrels of oil sent flames leaping three hundred feet into the air.

At Coney Island, the dance floor of the Moonlight Gardens was turned into a gigantic raft, and, at the peak of the flood, only the very top curves of the roller coasters were visible. The villages of New Richmond, Moscow, Nevills, and Point Pleasant were listed as being in dire need. Telephone service to these communities became difficult and sometimes impossible to supply.

The U.S. Coast Guard sent men, boats and airplanes to Cincinnati, where the National Red Cross had set up headquarters to direct relief efforts in all ten states. People brought and sent clothing, medicine, and trucks filled with rowboats from as far away as Dayton, Indianapolis, and Chicago.

On the showboat, each day we watched in awe the panorama of destruction that passed before us. The main channel was filled with drift from upriver: trees, barns, silos, empty barrels, boxes, furniture, roofs, and even whole houses. Anything that could float went racing by us in the furious current that carried everything in its wake.

Day and night, Dad, Leo, and Sam took turns standing on the front deck with a long pike pole, pushing away branches, logs, and other debris.

Animals, both wild and domestic, were caught by the deluge. Many were dead, but some were still living, swimming and spinning in circles like the mouse in *Alice in Wonderland,* holding their heads high with a wild look in their eyes.

Chickens flapped their wings and cackled and crowed from the tops of floating outbuildings. A squealing pig sailed by on a whole haystack, and a wet, sad-eyed calf, with drooping head, stood bawling on the side of an overturned privy.

Pets were a great part of my childhood, and at that time I had a Scottie named Duchess, a canary called Hamlet, and Patsy, a trained goat. The sight of those poor beasts in the water drove me frantic, and I spent hours sitting in the skiff, or rowboat, that was tied alongside, trying to reach some of them with an oar. I managed to bring several of the smaller creatures on board before Mother found me and dragged me to a safer location.

Several times the river stopped rising for a few hours, and even dropped a little at one point. But, it was merely toying with us. Before the flood would end, we would be tied to the very tip of that cottonwood tree and our auditorium would be filled with furniture and livestock belonging to victims of the deluge. Two sets of parlor furniture, several trunks filled with personal belongings, baskets of apples and barrels of pickles, jars of fruit and vegetables, and a beautiful canopy bed were piled on top of the seats.

On the stage we had a cow, two pigs, three sheep, and a goat. In the bacony and in the rafters were over a hundred chickens, several turkeys, a few ducks, and a pair of geese. When the flood was over and everything was gone, we found new meaning in the word "house-cleaning."

It was February 27 before the river dropped below flood stage at Cairo and the disaster was officially over. But it took another long month for the towns to clean up. Nevertheless, "come showboat time," they were ready and anxiously awaiting our arrival. Equally amazing was the fact that we were able in the same length of time to return our showboat to its former stature without a feather in sight.

Though I was most sympathetic to the people for what they had just experienced, it would have taken a bigger flood than the one in Johnstown to dampen my enthusiasm for the coming season.

I had just turned fifteen and was going to play ingenues and leading ladies. Goodbye Little Eva, so long, Little Willie, and, miracle of miracles, farewell, Mary Morgan. Well, two out of three wasn't bad.

We would be doing *Little Nell of the Ozarks*, *Lena Rivers*, *No Mother to Guide Her*, *The Gorilla*, *Over the Hill to the Poorhouse*, and *Tess of the Storm Country*.

I would still be doing my dance specialties, but now I would add monologues and a song that became so popular in Cincinnati people would ask when they made reservations, "Will Betty be singing *The Bird on Nellies Hat*?"

I truly loved doing the grown-up roles. In the next six years I would appear in *Agnes, the Switchman's Daughter*; *The Hatfields and the McCoys*; *Convict 999*; *Midnight in Chinatown*; *Bertha the Sewing Machine Girl*; *Nellie, the Beautiful Cloak Model*; *Trail of the Lonesome Pine*; *Tempest and Sunshine*; *Thorns and Orange Blossoms*; *Jack Dalton's Revenge*; and various other plays. But they weren't as easy as I had imagined.

When playing old melodramas like *Under the Bridge at Midnight*, *A Country Kid*, or *Her Dead Sister's Secret*, a dependable leading lady must be able to run, duck, fall, get up, fall again, crawl under a bed and over a dresser, scream, swing by a rope, deliver an uppercut, struggle and kick, and still have enough breath left to say, "If this is aristocracy, thank *God* I'm a country girl!"

I was confined in madhouses, prisons, graves, huts, caves, trunks, castles, toolsheds, grandfather clocks, and opium dens.

I was pursued by gangsters, magicians, dope fiends, bull fighters, squatters, maniacs, assassins, gypsies, and chinamen, not to mention a goodly assortment of suave villains.

I have been kidnapped, stabbed, shot, poisoned, beaten, doped, buried alive, and sold down the river. I have been tied to a log and

Betty singing "The Bird on Nellie's Hat"

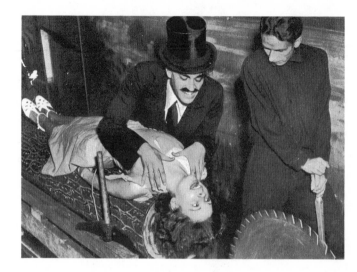

The
sawmill
scene in
*Jack
Dalton's
Revenge*

Betty, playing the
lead in *Carmen*, is
threatened by
Escamillo
(Gordon Ray)

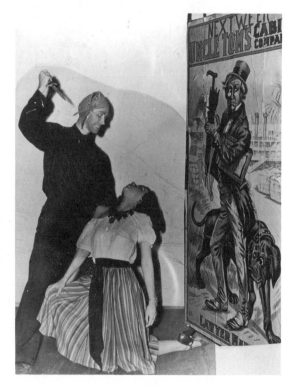

A typical archvillain (Doug
Morris) making unwelcome
advances on the heroine (Betty)

After kidnapping Fanny
(Betty), Jack Dalton (Milton
Haskins) and his henchman
Willie (Gordon Ray) spirit her
through town to the sawmill

Betty applies makeup before a show

pushed head first toward a grinding buzz saw, I have been slung over a gorilla's shoulder and hauled off the balcony, and I have been lashed to a railroad track while three actors ran over me pulling a huge train made of canvas.

Almost every season Dad would get at least one letter from some young woman who dreamed of being the leading lady on a showboat. But once he got me broken in, he never even considered anyone else. He said once that leading ladies in melodrama had to be tough, and it was best to get 'em young, feed 'em well, and keep 'em in good condition.

In 1939, we were at Portsmouth when I had to have an appendectomy. I went to the hospital and had the operation. We were playing *Tess of the Storm Country*. I was doing Tess in the show and a soft shoe dance as a specialty.

I was in the hospital for two weeks, during which time Mother played Tess. The evening I came home, Mother took me into the ticket office and gave me the high stool to sit on while I sold tickets.

Dad came into the office and practically danced. "Oh, great, honey!" he said and kissed me on the cheek. "You can do the soft-shoe tonight." Mother hit the roof!

"What are you talking about? This child has had a serious operation. She just got home today. You must be out of your mind! She certainly will not be able to do the soft-shoe!"

Dad smiled at me and put his hands on my shoulders. Leaning into my face he said, "Honey, if you can walk, you can dance!" I did. And I have been ever since.

WHERE HAVE ALL THE
SHOWBOATS GONE?

Except for a pause during the Civil War, showboats traveled the rivers for over a hundred years as an integral part of our cultural history. They reached their zenith a little after the turn of the century. They came into existence to meet the early settlers' demand for formal entertainment, and they disappeared when the need was gone.

A few of them operated into the early 1940s, but one by one they disappeared. Some were sold, to be converted into wharf boats or floating clubhouses, others were dismantled and broken up for firewood. A few were beached to lie among the willows like giant skeletons of white whales, their wooden bones bleaching in the summer sun.

In 1943, Dad sold our showboat to a freight terminal company in Huntington, West Virginia. In one last salute to sentiment, he insisted upon a clause being inserted in the contract stating the boat would never again be used as a showboat. The romantic shell lay idle at the wharf for six years. Then, during a flood, it sank to the bottom of the Ohio River.

Two of the inland waterways giants remain, but they do not travel. In 1937, the *Goldenrod* took permanent mooring at the landing at St. Louis, Missouri. It has been registered as a National Historic Landmark, placed on a steel barge, and is still in operation as a supper club.

THE END OF THE OLD BILLY BRYANT SHOW BOAT at the foot of Tenth street, is a matter of
a few weeks. Only a portion of the boat, which sank a few days before Christmas, was visible
above the high waters of the flooding Ohio River yesterday. The boat will be scrapped when the
water rec▪des, its owner announced. (Staff Photo)

* * *   * * *

High Water Is Graveyard
For Bryant's Old Showboat

By MARGARET W. NEFF

High water this past w e e k
spelled the end of the historic
old Billy Bryant Show B o a t,
which sank at its mooring at the
foot of Tenth street just before
Christmas. Grayson Thornton,
principal stockholder of the
Huntington Terminal Company
which owns the boat, said that
efforts to raise the boat h a d
been stymied by r e p e a t e d
rises of the water. Yesterday,
only a portion of the u p p e r
deck was visible a b o v e the
swirling waters of the O h i o
river.

Mr. Thornton said when the
water recedes, the old s h ow
boat, once a mecca for lovers
of old - fashioned melodrama,
will be hauled ashore and dismantled into scrap lumber.

Plans to use the b o a t as a
freight terminal, the purpose for
which the Huntington Terminal
Company was formed by Mr.

Thornton, Tom Harvey and Mrs.
Thornton, have been abandoned
as unprofitable, he s a i d. Mr.
Thornton, however, will m a i n-
tain his lease of the T e n t h
street landing site, where he
also operates the Waste Paper
Packing Company.

The Bryant Show Boat h a s
been tied up at the Tenth street
landing for the past six years,
and for a time served as a wharf
boat for smaller privately-
owned craft. Prior to that time,
the site was used by the Greene
Lines wharf boat, which at one
time handled a large flow of
freight carried by packets up
and down the river.

Mr. Thornton said t h a t a
thorough investigation of t h e
freight situation had convinced
his company that the cost of
maintaining a wharf boat at the
Tenth street landing w o u l d
make handling of freight unprofitable.

At Cincinnati, the *Majestic*, originally owned by the Reynolds family, lies at the foot of Broadway, offering contemporary plays on board. It has been kept in its original form and is a beautiful example of a true Floating Theater. It too is a National Historic Landmark.

Now and again, some enterprising resort owner will advertise a showboat with entertainment on board. They are great fun to visit but are usually small, self-propelled boats, often with an ornamental stern wheel paddle. The interior is furnished with tables and chairs and sometimes a bar. Refreshments and a boat ride are the main attractions, with entertainment added seemingly as an afterthought.

But the genuine touring showboat, built between 1830 and 1930, is gone forever. Like so many examples of early Americanna, it outlived its usefulness and took its place in line behind the covered wagon and the keel boat.

In 1942, when our boats closed, Dad bought a home in Point Pleasant where Violet and Sam retired. Dad went on to do shows in New York and Chicago, to write, direct, lecture, and make appearances at fairs and expositions. He was in constant demand as a radio and television guest, and he played the part of the owner of the livery stable in a movie called *The Missouri Traveler*, starring Lee Marvin.

In 1947, Dad was called to the West Coast, ostensibly for a consultation on a play he had written. On arrival, he found himself to be the guest star on Ralph Edwards's radio show "This Is your Life."

Mother, my husband, my four-year-old daughter, and I were spirited out to Hollywood. The other two people on the show were Mack Franks, a showboat actor from the early days and Buster Keaton's mother, Myra, who had worked on the Bryant's Medicine Show.

Ralph Edwards greeted us graciously and showed us the script. He asked me if I would be willing to do a short scene as—who else?—Mary Morgan. I paused, and then suggested that my daughter do it as a fourth-generation performer. He agreed, and in fifteen minutes I taught her to sing, "Father, dear Father, come home with me now!"

That night, as her sweet little voice sent those lyrics out over the airwaves, I thought, rather smugly, that I had at last finished with that character. "Oh, the best laid plans of mice and men!"

Sam lived to be ninety-two years old, and Violet passed away a little over a year after his death. She must have been close to ninety, but when the attending physician asked her age, she smiled, patted her freshly dyed curls and said, "Oh, doctor, you know 'ow we theater people feel about telling 'ow old we are. 'owever, since you *are* a professional man, oy will tell *you* my age. Hit's 62!" I'm sure she died happy.

Dad never really retired, but, after the death of his parents, he and Mother moved to Florida. In 1968, within three months of one another Captain Menke of the *Goldenrod Showboat*, Edna Ferber, author of the book *Show Boat*, and my father, Captain Billy Bryant, passed away.

Two years later, Florence, the last of the Four Bryants, died. They are all buried in Point Pleasant. My mother, Josephine, passed away in 1972.

In 1978, when the Smithsonian Institution, in Washington, D.C., opened its new Maritime Wing, a model to scale of the *Bryant's Showboat* and the steamer *Valley Belle* were placed on permanent display as a "genuine, if whimsical part of the history of the inland waterways of the United States." Dad would have been very proud.

In 1981, I was invited to Washington, D.C., to take part in the Smithsonian Institution's Fifteenth Annual Festival of American Folklife, specifically in that part of the festival known as the Celebration of the American Tent Show.

I spent two weeks working under canvas with representatives of minstrel shows, medicine shows, rep shows, tent shows, and chautauquas. We did nineteen shows and lectures and changed material as much as possible. Everything was videotaped to be placed in the archives of the Smithsonian Institution for students or writers to refer to.

I did a buck and wing, soft-shoe, sand dance, and waltz clog. I played Tess in a scene from *Tess of the Storm Country*, and, of course, Mary Morgan's first scene in *Ten Nights in a Barroom*, So, at the age of fifty-nine, with my long hair hanging down my back and a worn shawl over my head, I led Joe Morgan across the stage while singing,

> Father, dear Father, come home with me now.
> The clock in the steeple strikes one.
> You promised, dear Father, that you would come home
> As soon as your day's work was done.
> Come home! Come home!
> Dear Father, dear Father, come home!

As we made our exit to thunderous applause, I suddenly realized that, for me, there was no escape from Mary Morgan. And I really didn't mind. Since then, I have written of her, directed her in community theater, and found myself remembering good times we shared. It's not likely that we will work together again in this world, but I wouldn't mind if we did. She was a nice character.

In the summer of 1991, I returned to Point Pleasant to perform for two days on the Always a River Museum Barge. I was there under the sponsorship of the WVFWC Point Pleasant Junior Woman's Club, and I stayed with Charles and Lily Faye Lanham. A more gracious couple I have never met. Georgiana Tillis was my devoted guide and assistant.

When I first arrived in Point Pleasant, the barge had not yet arrived. I walked down the cobblestone landing to look at the beautiful river. In my mind I could almost see a showboat gliding along in the middle of the channel, and I seemed to hear the ghosts of melodies that had been blasted through those hills by the screech of long-gone calliopes.

Soon the barge came in and I went on board. One end of the museum housed a pleasant little indicative theater named *Betty Bryant's New Showboat*. It held a small stage and enough seats for thirty or forty people. At the entryway stood a lifesize cutout of Callie French of *French's New Sensation*, and, through the kindness of Rita Kohn, the project coordinator, around the stage the walls were covered with pictures of *Bryant's Showboat* and Donald McDaniel's chronological list of all the showboats down through the years. Exhibit visitors along the 981-mile route put on costumes to perform my specially written four-character five-minute script, *If Jack Were Only Here*.

In the two days, five thousand people came on board. I gave fourteen performances, talking, singing, and dancing, and, between shows, I answered questions, posed for pictures, and greeted and visited with old friends, particularly dear Catherine Reynolds and her brothers of the *Majestic Showboat*.

After my last show, I went up the bank to the park and watched an excellent program entitled "Life Along the River," presented by the Point Pleasant High School speech team. The students portrayed historical characters from the Ohio River Valley. They were all wonderful, and Matt Wedge, wearing my father's hat on loan from the Point Pleasant Historical Society, played my father to the hilt. He brought such youthful verve to the role, I found myself waiting for him to break into a buck and wing.

A fireworks display, purposely set up on the opposite side of the river, closed the day's events. As the rockets soared and burst over the trees, their reflection in the water doubled the beauty of the airborne display. Dozens of children stood on the bank, wide-eyed and clinging to their parent's hands. For just a fleeting moment I felt sad. Those children, like countless others are being deluged with mechanical toys. Machines sing for them, dance for them, juggle for them, and even laugh for them. They were born to the sound of canned music and are growing up clustered around television sets that spew out secondhand dreams. They will be more informed, amused, entertained, and catered to than any other children in the history of the world.

But if I could have had only one wish that night I would have turned back the clock just long enough to let them thrill to the shrill voice of a small boy high in a cottonwood tree, waving his hat in the air and promising the wonders of the world with the cry of

"HERE COMES THE SHOOOOOOOOOOOOOOOWBOAT!!!!!"

SHOWBOAT CHRONOLOGY

1831	*Chapman's Floating Theatre*
1832	*Chapman's Floating Theatre*
1833	*Chapman's Floating Theatre*
1834	*Chapman's Floating Theatre*
1835	*Chapman's Floating Theatre*
1836-50	*Butler's Museum Boat*
1836-47	*Steamboat Theatre* (later *Chapman's Floating Palace*)
1842-48?	*Jersey City Show Barge*
1845-48?	*Temple of the Muses*
?-1849	*Lennox Theatre* (later *Rough and Ready*)
1853-66	*James Raymond*
1855-61	*Banjo*
1856-?	*Buhoup's Great Floating Hindoo Pagoda*
1864-?	*Ward's Floating Theatre*
1878-87	*The New Sensation*
1881-?	*Bird's Floating Opera House*
1886-?	*Rice's Floating Opera*
1887-94	*French's New Sensation* (later *Voyager Co.*)
1888-91	*Price's Floating Opera*
1888-1900	*Robinson's Floating Palace and Grand Opera House* (later *New Marine Exhibition* and *French's New Sensation No. 2*)

1889-1900	*Eisenbarth's Combined Wild West and Opera* (later *Price's Floating Opera* and *David Garrick*)
1889-91	*Hughes Floating Enterprise*
1889-1900?	*New Floating Theatorium* (later *French's New Sensation No. 1* and *New Olympia*)
1889-?	*Paden's New Crystal Palace*
1890?-1905	*Twentieth Century*
1896-99	*Floating Star Theatre*
1899-1902	*Eisenbarth and Henderson Modern Temple of Amusement*
1900-1917	*Lightner's Floating Palace* (later *New Era*)
1901-31	*French's New Sensation*
1901-?	*Great Southern Showboat*
1901-17	*New Grand Floating Palace* (later *Emerson's Floating Palace* and *Greater New York*)
1901-38	*Price's New Water Queen* (later *Greater Pittsburgh*, *Water Queen*, and *Cotton Blossom No. 2*)
1903-18	*Eisenbarth and Henderson New Modern Temple of Amusement* (later *Cotton Blossom*)
1905-16?	*Dreamland*
1905-6?	*Gent Showboat*
1905-19?	*Sunny South* (later *Hippodrome*)
1906-18?	*Wonderland*
1907-28	*Princess*
1909-present	*Markle's New Showboat* (later *Goldenrod*)
1910-16	*Illinois*
1911-39	*American* (later *Columbia* and *Hollywood*)
1914-16	*Dixie*
1914-41	*James Adams Floating Theatre* (later *Original Showboat* and *Original Floating Theatre*)
1917-33	*America*
1918-42	*Bryant's New Showboat*
1918-23	*Cotton Blossom Pavilion*
1918-29	*River Maid*

1918-23?	Superior
1921-?	Modern
1922-?	Drake's Floating Movie
1922-?	Rex
1922-?	Sunny South
1922-30	Water Lilly
1923-present	Majestic
1923-24	Peerless
1924-32	Cotton Blossom
1924-32	Gayety (later Valley)
1925-30s	Bear Mountain
1927-29	Bart's Big Fun Show
1932-34	Cotton Blossom
1932-37	Dixiana
1933-40	Buccaneer
1933-38	Horicon
1933-36	Paradise Showboat
1939-45	Dixie Queen
1940-43	Cotton Blossom
1956-75	Point Counterpoint
1958-present	Minnesota Centennial Showboat
1962-present	Driftwood Floating Theatre
1963-present	Showboat Rhododendron (later City of Clinton)
1974	Alabama Belle
1975-present	Becky Thatcher
1976-84	Nashville Showboat
1976-present	Point Counterpoint II
1977-present	Golden Eagle
1985-present	General Jackson

Note: This chronology was compiled by Donald McDaniel, editor and publisher of the newsletter *Showboat Centennials*. The chronology is updated frequently, as information on showboats is uncovered. A current, and more detailed, chronology may be obtained for $2 (to cover printing and shipping costs) from Showboat Centennials, 76 Glen Drive, Worthington, OH 43085.

FOR FURTHER INFORMATION

The Showboat Centennials at Worthington, Ohio, under the dedicated guidance of Donald McDaniel, has amassed an enormous amount of interesting and notable facts regarding the showboat era.

Ralph DuPae of La Crosse, Wisconsin, has done a remarkable job of furthering the University of Wisconsin's formidable collection of riverboat photographs.

Point Pleasant, West Virginia, has a river museum in progress, and the Smithsonian Institution in Washington, D.C., as well as the Mississippi River Museum in Memphis, has a model of the *Bryant's Showboat* on display.

In the Woodward Riverboat Museum at Dubuque, Iowa, a new wing devotes one large room to showboat memorabillia. They have over ninety artifacts from the *Bryant's Showboat* alone.

In 1991 the Always a River Museum Barge, towed by the American Electric Power Company's boat, the *Boonesboro*, toured from Pittsburgh to Cairo, stopping at twenty-one towns on the way for stays of from two days to two weeks. Each town contributed to the project with pageants, speakers, fireworks displays, parades, and new museums. The project was funded through a National Endowment for the Humanities Exemplary Grant in conjunction with the humanities counsels of the six Ohio River states. Its object was to show the significance of the Ohio River in the larger American story. The showboat, born in Pittsburgh of British theater stock, is a recognized American original. Regional theater in America can be traced to showboat roots. The Always a River exhibit was removed from the barge at summer's end in 1991. It will be permanently housed in the new museum in Clarksville, Indiana, overlooking the Falls of the Ohio.

INDEX